P   cial   and

Bilingualism

Bilingualism

Social Issues and Policy Implications

ANDREW W. MIRACLE, JR., EDITOR

Southern Anthropological Society Proceedings, No. 16
Robert L. Blakely, Series Editor

The University of Georgia Press
Athens, Georgia 30602

Southern Anthropological Society

Founded 1966

OFFICERS 1981–1982

Elizabeth M. Eddy, President
Malcolm C. Webb, President-Elect
David M. Johnson, Secretary-Treasurer
Patricia D. Beaver, Councilor
Louise M. Robbins, Councilor
Mary W. Helms, Councilor
Robert L. Blakely, Series Editor
Nancy H. Owen, Newsletter Editor

Program Coordinator, 1982:
Gregory Reck

Copyright © 1983 by the Southern Anthropological Society
All rights reserved

Set in 11 on 13 point Times Roman type
Printed in the United States of America

The paper in this book meets the guidelines for permanence and durability of the Committee on Production Guidelines for Book Longevity of the Council on Library Resources.

Library of Congress Cataloging in Publication Data

Main entry under title:
Bilingualism, social issues and policy implications.
   (Southern Anthropological Society proceedings; no. 16)
   Includes papers presented in a symposium of the 16th annual meeting of the Southern Anthropological Society, Fort Worth, Texas, April 1981.
   Bibliography: p.
   1. Bilingualism—Congresses. 2. Language policy—Congresses. 3. Education, Bilingual—Congresses. I. Miracle, Andrew W. II. Southern Anthropological Society. Meeting (16th : 1981 : Fort Worth, Tex.)
III. Series.
GN2.S9243 no. 16 [P115]   301S [306'.4]   82–13447
ISBN 0–8203–0645–2
ISBN 0–8203–0646–0 (pbk.)

Contents

Foreword

Once relegated to academic discourse among anthropologists and linguists, bilingualism today is not an uncommon news item. Resistance to acculturation and heightened ethnic awareness as well as advances in sociolinguistics have led to widespread recognition of the critical role that bilingualism plays in enculturation, ethnicity, education, and even self-identity. And the significance of bilingualism has not been lost on educators, community planners, and national and international policy makers of many ilks throughout the world. In the United States, the social and economic implications of bilingual education have been argued before the Supreme Court. The challenge to anthropologists is clear: because the data we generate and the conclusions we reach influence policy decisions, studies of bilingualism must be well reasoned, couched in sound data, and tempered by compassion.

The contributions to this volume constitute an important step in that direction. While grounded in traditional sociolinguistic theory, they offer innovative approaches to the topical issue of bilingualism. Most of the authors originally presented their papers in the Key Symposium of the 16th annual meeting of the Southern Anthropological Society in Fort Worth, Texas, in April, 1981. Special thanks for assembling this collection of scholars go to Andy Miracle. His enthusiasm, organization, and attention to details have made my job as editor easier. And I am grateful to Robert A. Rubinstein for his careful review of the manuscripts. This work has benefited enormously from Bob's insights.

As I end my stint as editor of the SAS Proceedings, I wish to thank the many people who assisted me in this task. I was fortunate to work with volume editors Tom Collins, Bob Hall and Carol Stack, and Andy Miracle, who were dedicated to scholarship, diligent, attentive to deadlines, and always personable. Karen Orchard, managing editor of the University of Georgia Press, advised and coaxed while exercising remarkable forbearance. To my successor, Mary Helms, I offer best wishes and my condolences.

Robert L. Blakely
SAS Proceedings Editor

Preface

The articles contained in this volume represent eleven attempts to address social issues and policy implications related to bilingualism. As the articles illustrate, there are many tacks that one may take in this regard. The variety of perspectives exhibited by the authors reflects the reality of dealing with bilingualism in the contemporary world—whether as researcher, student, teacher, policy maker, administrator, or an individual living in an environment that is not monolingual. Accordingly, this volume should have utility for a wide-ranging audience. It has been my intention in this volume to present articles that would be of interest and benefit to such an audience.

The articles included in this volume address many of the most pressing issues in the study and application of research in bilingualism. Serious students and professionals may be stimulated by the new data and theoretical concerns presented here. However, every effort has been made to limit technical jargon and to promote clarity, so that beginning students and lay persons might benefit from the presentations.

The issues discussed in this volume are too important to be left solely to anthropologists, linguists, and applied social scientists. Today bilingualism or multilingualism touches, at least indirectly, the overwhelming majority of people. Therefore, all have a right—indeed an obligation—to be informed in order to effect appropriate decisions regarding this global phenomenon.

Bob Blakely deserves credit for having the foresight three years ago to suggest the organization of a symposium on bilingualism. Except for his wisdom and encouragement, this volume might never have been. Mary Helms, President of the Southern Anthropological Society, also guided me and provided necessary support. Special recognition is due Bill Ray, who graciously prepared the map on Philippines Region IX.

Mostly, however, I am indebted to those who participated in the symposium. Those who read papers, chaired sessions, listened attentively, and asked probing questions all helped to create a successful symposium. The papers published in these proceedings represent only a portion of the participatory efforts that constituted the symposium. I especially wish to thank Nora England. Her discussion of the papers at the time of the meeting was incisive and aided both authors and audience. In addition, the introduction that she provided for this volume should greatly assist readers in organizing ideas before commencing with the articles as well as provide an analytical framework for evaluating the articles later.

I also wish to express my indebtedness to Texas Christian University and the Department of Sociology for the assistance provided to the Southern Anthropological Society in regard to the 1981 meeting in Fort Worth. In no small part, my colleagues at TCU made this volume possible. Finally, I wish to thank Phyllis Drake for her aid in preparations for the symposium as well as in final preparation of this manuscript.

Andrew W. Miracle, Jr.

Bilingualism

Introduction

Nora C. England

Scholarly interest in bilingualism and language contact has a solid history of achievement in the past four decades. Classic studies by Uriel Weinreich and Einar Haugen lead the field and have provided the inspiration for a substantial amount of subsequent work, but there have been many other illustrious scholars engaged in the field. Far from exhausting the possibilities for research in bilingualism, these years have served to define problems of interest, to eliminate some futile avenues of inquiry, to begin to provide adequate theoretical approaches to bilingualism, and to develop data against which to test those theories. The past decade has seen a rapid expansion of programs for bilingual education in almost all areas of the world, which has resulted in a new emphasis on the applications of knowledge about bilingualism to educational planning and national language policy.

This volume contains a collection of articles on bilingualism and bilingual education that are by and large the result of very recent research by relatively young scholars. All of the authors have in common that their research has been with bilinguals; for most of them, the research has taken place within the context of implementing or evaluating language policy decisions. The volume therefore reflects the new emphases and directions of the past ten years, in which governments, schools, teachers, parents, and scholars have met in the exciting but difficult and frustrating task of formulating policies that recognize the existence of bilingual populations within state and community boundaries. The individual papers in the volume deal with a wide variety of themes that, although they by no means exhaust the topics of current interest in bilingualism research, include the following: languages in contact (Collins, Painter); national policy regarding bilingualism (DeCicco and Maring, Randall, Stark, Briggs, Carpenter, Kephart); definitions of bilingualism (Kephart); the effectiveness of bilingual education programs (Stark, Randall, Briggs, Carpenter, Cohen); new research on bilingualism (Blount); and internal and external evaluation of bilingual education programs (Cohen, Miller and Cárdenas).

The specific mechanisms of change that occur when languages are in contact, especially nonphonological change, still need documentation. Collins' paper describes a semantic change in the Spanish translation of Aymara affinal terminology, and shows how such shifts must be reckoned with in interpreting the languages of peoples in contact. The paper points out one of the mechanisms whereby minority languages can have a substantial effect on majority languages—through bilingual translation conventions. It also underscores the point that when languages are in contact many of the ways in which they accommodate each other occur through a group of real individuals who are bilingual in the languages concerned. Further, much of the popular evidence for deficiency models of language ability comes directly out of the translation situation that Collins describes. In spite of considerable linguistic and sociolinguistic work that has convincingly challenged such models (for example, the work of William Labov, especially Labov 1969), it is apparently not redundant to address them once again.

For the same community in Peru that Collins describes, where Spanish and Aymara are the languages in contact, Painter examines definitions of ethnicity as they are related to language and economic factors, using a distinctive feature analysis of social categories. This topic is fascinating for Latin America, where theoretical battles about ethnicity rage around the issues of class versus caste and where Indians and non-Indians are often defined, at least analytically and from the outside, on the basis of language. Recent work has shown that although outsiders tend to define Indians in Latin America as people who speak an indigenous American language, the group so defined may not find that definition appropriate (Friedlander 1975), and there are ethnic groups that cannot be defined in such simple terms (Stocks 1978). Language use in many areas is a consequence of ethnicity rather than a definition of it, and patterns of language use frequently shift. The situation Painter describes in Moho is enormously interesting within the context of the literature on ethnicity for Latin America because he analyzes three separate groups of people all of whom speak (at least potentially) the two languages of the area. Follow-up research on sociolinguistic patterns of language use in the area could contribute to studies of ethnicity as well as language contact research.

DeCicco and Maring compare Spain and the Philippines with regard to national language policy, and provide substantial detail about the actual language structure and attitudes in the two nations. They point out the importance of history and of the interplay between ethnicity, national identity, and international identity in the emergence of national language decisions. This paper, as well as those of Collins and Painter, highlights the importance of language and identity factors at different levels of interaction.

Randall's paper addresses the results of national language policy in one region of the Philippines, and therefore provides a case within the background of DeCicco and Maring's discussion. In addition to pointing out problems of implementing national language policy in a country with great language and ethnic diversity, Randall makes an especially important distinction with regard to the intent of bilingual policy in different nations. The United States, at least sometimes and recently, has instituted bilingual education and other bilingual services (such as public signs, driver's exams) for the purpose of expanding opportunities and services to be available to a wider population, not limited by the native language. The Philippines, on the other hand, has instituted a bilingual policy the effect of which is to limit the availability of opportunities and services to only those people who speak the languages that have been made official. A number of other papers in this volume, notably that by Stark, provide other evidence that language policy can be distinctly limiting in intent.

Stark reports on research in Paraguay the goal of which was to test various alphabets prior to attempting a bilingual education program in Guaraní. The test methodology she reports is very useful. An astonishing number of programs to teach literacy in languages that do not have a standard alphabet neglect to do any research on the ease of learning or using a practical orthography. Further, the question of an alphabet, when there is a choice, is almost universally a serious political and emotional problem, and decisions about adopting an alphabet must take these factors into account. Stark's paper is also an instructive case of stillbirth in bilingual education, due to policy rather than to practice.

Almost anyone who has been involved in implementing a bilingual education program has experienced at one time or another failure and problems of morale. Briggs documents a recent Bolivian attempt at bilingual education that encountered almost every problem that plagues such programs, including lack of planning, lack of teacher preparation, lack of teacher/community involvement, late staffing, cultural misunderstanding, contradictory policy, and lack of government support at crucial junctures. Briggs makes very sensible suggestions, and her paper is a warning against too much idealism. At the same time, it points out that it is not necessary to give up in the face of adversity.

Carpenter addresses one of the problems that bilingual education programs often face—that of different levels of support within the community. He points out that in Ecuador, at least, the assumption that speakers of Quichua are a homogeneous group is false. An analysis of cultural and linguistic factors shows that there are different classes within the Quichua population and that these have different, but predictable, reactions to bilingual education. This is an extremely important point, one that all planners in bilingual education should, but often fail to, take into account. Carpenter's paper, like Painter's, also deals with the relationship between language and ethnicity.

Kephart's paper, unlike the others in this section, discusses the language problems of an area where bilingualism is not recognized. He shows that definitions of bilingualism, in a very practical sense, are needed and are not clear-cut, and makes a good case for English/Creole bilingualism on Carriacou. He suggests bilingual education for teaching "Export English," realizing that great shifts of attitude need to be effected to implement such a program successfully. The other papers in the section show just how difficult such shifts in attitude may be. A valuable point in Kephart's paper is showing that a deficiency model of language ability is very strong on Carriacou, and is applied to Creole speakers by both themselves and others. More politicking on this point is in order.

There are certainly many areas of interest for research in bilingualism and bilingual education that have yet to be undertaken. Blount suggests new research in the area of extralinguistic features of bilingualism, and presents a study of Spanish- and English-speaking parents that compares their extralinguistic features in speaking to young children. I think that as a corollary to the sort of research that Blount proposes it also would be important to investigate teaching strategies that could attack the learning of extralinguistic features of a second language, rather than assuming that second-language students will pick them up. While research in this area is not entirely lacking, it is the rare bilingual education program that formally incorporates it into the program.

Another aspect of research on bilingualism is program evaluation of bilingual education projects, both internal and external. Cohen's suggestions for internal program evaluation are both lucid and positive. Such guides can be invaluable to teachers and evaluators. Anyone who thinks of starting a new bilingual education program would do well to investigate evaluative procedures as well as teaching methods and materials development.

Miller and Cárdenas' paper is also a useful guide to evaluation, from the viewpoint of external U.S. government mandated and funded evaluation of the programs it sponsors. These two papers on evaluation point out that there are different kinds of evaluation of bilingual education with somewhat different purposes. One thing we want to know is how bilingual education works in theory and practice; another type of evaluation deals essentially with continued funding of projects and government policy toward such projects. These overlap somewhat, but are not entirely compatible. Responsible evaluation is necessary, however, in order to find out how effective bilingual education in different situations can be, to discover which social, cultural, pedagogical, and linguistic factors affect the success of the programs, and to make policy decisions on such matters as funding and continuation.

All of the papers in this volume contain some common underlying assumptions. One is that the social and linguistic factors that apply in bilingual situations are so complex that they warrant further research, case studies, and policy reviews. Another is that bilingual education is a reasonable way of extending educational opportunity in bilingual regions. Since a relatively large number of the papers point out moderate to severe problems in extant or defunct bilingual education programs, it is reasonable to ask why this faith in bilingual education persists. It was pointed out in the discussion of the papers at the SAS Key Symposium that in many cases bilingual education has not gone nearly far enough. Part of the reason for failure has been inadequate government or community commitment to such programs and an unwillingness to give them even a minimal opportunity to prove themselves. I think that most of the authors would agree that bilingual education programs should be extended and strengthened, always bearing in mind the sorts of problems that have been mentioned in their papers and trying to work out solutions to them.

Part One

Bilingualism in Community and State

Translation Traditions and the Organization of Productive Activity: The Case of Aymara Affinal Kinship Terms

JANE COLLINS

The Aymara of the district of Moho, department of Puno, in southern Peru, possess a complex terminology for the marking of affinal kin. The terminology denotes the many-stranded alliance relationships between two households whose members marry. These relationships are among the most highly valued in Aymara society. They delineate obligations of respect and assistance, and organize work activities and exchanges of labor and goods.

In recent years native affinal kinship terms have been increasingly replaced by Spanish terminology. Spanish terms have their origins in a system of affinal relations whose structural characteristics are very different from those of the Aymara system. Thus, the way in which they are employed by native speakers of Aymara is different from the way they are employed, for example, by native speakers of coastal Peruvian Spanish. (See Escobar 1978 for an explanation of the different varieties of Spanish spoken in Peru.) Their usage does not reflect the Spanish system of affinal kinship, but reflects an attempt to preserve the social and economic relationships of the Aymara affinal system, under different names.

This paper explores the way in which translation traditions function for the rendering of Aymara concepts into Spanish. It examines how these traditions allow the maintenance of the behavioral categories of the native Aymara kinship system. First, the Aymara system and its terms will be described. Then, the Spanish system and terms will be briefly presented. Finally, the way in which Spanish terms are used to express Aymara concepts will be discussed.

THE AYMARA AFFINAL SYSTEM

Edmund Leach has said: "There are two kinds of marriage. The first results from the whims of two persons acting as private individuals; the second is a systematically organized affair which forms part of a series of contractual obligations between two social groups." (1951:24.) Aymara marriage is nearly always of the second variety. It is an economic union between three household units in which the family of the man and the family of the woman incur mutual obligations toward one another at the same time that the newly married couple incurs obligations toward both sets of parents and siblings.

The nuclear family household has often been described as the basic unit of Andean and Aymara kinship. It is true that virtually every couple establishes an independent productive unit within a few years of marriage. But while the new household is responsible for the making of productive decisions and allocation of its own resources, it is still bound by numerous ties and obligations to the families from which it emerged.

The long series of wedding ceremonies described by Carter (1977) symbolically ties the newlyweds to their spouses' families. It also creates very real obligations by the provision of land, seed, animals, and other resources. An Aymara couple enter their productive life surrounded by networks of commitments and responsibilities. As Carter says, "by the time the ceremonial sequence has been completed, couples have so many social obligations to kindred of bride, groom, and godparents, that they will be involved in lending and borrowing of goods and services for the rest of their lives" (1977:210).

Because of the complexity and the long-term nature of the obligations they incur, Aymara marriages are not easily dissolved. Divorces in Aymara communities are rare occurrences, and are often negatively sanctioned by the families of the couple who dissolve their marriage. Because the commitments formed in the marriage process involve several family groups and a large number of people, only a clear-cut refusal to abide by those commitments, and not the whims or desires of individuals, is sufficient basis to end the relationship. It is also for this reason that, in the case of the death of a spouse, the sororate and levirate are often practiced.

At the most basic level, the obligations incurred by the act of marriage in Aymara society stem from the removal of a productive member from his or her household. The valued labor capacities of that individual become unavailable to the household that has nurtured them. Therefore this household must demand reciprocation for the investment its members have made. This aspect of alliance systems has often been recognized in the anthropological literature (Lévi-Strauss 1969; Leach 1951; Goody 1976; Meillassoux 1975), but analysis has most often been limited to the exchange, by men, of the labor capacities of women.

For the Aymara, the productive capacities of the sexes are equally valued. Furthermore, the control over a household's labor does not lie in the hands of its male members. Productive decisions are the result of consensus among all members of the household. Thus, a domestic unit that gives up a son or a brother to the formation of a new household is structurally equivalent to a domestic unit that gives up a daughter or sister. In both cases, the group that provides the potential worker is entitled to receive deferent behavior and goods and services from the new family.

Obviously, this arrangement creates networks of obligations that are both symmetrical and asymmetrical. A son-in-law is always subordinate to his wife's relatives, in the same way that a daughter-in-law is subordinate to her husband's. At the level of the parent families, however, the obligations become balanced and reciprocal, for both sets of parents have contributed a productive member to the formation of the new household. It is these symmetries and asymmetries in the obligations incurred by marriage that are marked by the Aymara affinal terminology.

The term *yuqch'a*, for example, can be glossed as either "son's wife" or "brother's wife." Both of these people are husband-takers in relation to the family that raised the man in question. The relations of the yuqch'a to that family are ordered around the recognition that their son or brother is now producing for her. The mirror image of this term is *tullqa*. A tullqa is the husband of a daughter or of a sister. He is seen as a wife-taker, and owes the corresponding respect to the family of the woman he marries. To approach the relationships from a different angle, the sister of one's husband is known as *ipala*. The ipala is a husband-giver to her yuqch'a. The

brother of one's wife is a *lari* or wife-giver to his respective tullqa.
(See Figure 1.)

These categories appear to have structural equivalents in other
parts of the Andes. Mayer (1977) and Isbell (1978) have described
the *masa/llumchuy* (*masha/llumtschuy*) relationship for Tangor in
Pasco and Chuschi in Ayacucho. These categories appear to be similar
to those of tullqa and yuqch'a in Aymara. Webster (1977) and Zuidema (1977) have discovered similarly structured arrangements of
affinal kin in Cuzco. In all of these cases, the tullqa and yuqch'a
categories are viewed as outsiders to the nuclear family group of
their lari and ipala. This is also the case among the Aymara of
Moho. Furthermore, as in Moho, the tullqa and yuqch'a categories
have important obligations toward their spouses' families.

Figure 1. Diagrams for Aymara Affinal Kin

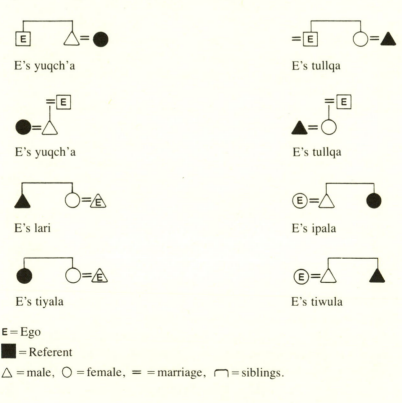

E's yuqch'a   E's tullqa

E's yuqch'a   E's tullqa

E's lari   E's ipala

E's tiyala   E's tiwula

E = Ego

■ = Referent

△ = male, ○ = female, = = marriage, ⌐ = siblings.

A further characteristic that Aymara affinal terminology has in common with similar systems observed in Quechua-speaking areas is the fact that once affinal categories are established they are extended to the consanguineal kin involved. Thus the tullqa acquires his status by marrying someone's daughter or sister, but the woman, upon marriage to him, also becomes a tullqa with relation to her own family, as do her offspring. A man acquires the status of yuqch'a with relation to his own family when he marries and brings a yuqch'a into the family structure. It is important to note that only in these types of extensions to consanguineal relatives, which occur in a limited number of situations, can the ordinarily sex-specific affinal terms cross sex lines.

THE SPANISH AFFINAL SYSTEM

The Spanish system for categorizing affinal kin is much less complex than the one just described for the Aymara. Rather than concerning itself with specifying who owes what to whom in a marriage contract, the Spanish system is concerned with the setting apart of relatives by blood from those who acquire their status by marriage only. Thus, a *cuñado* (brother-in-law) is someone who has acquired a status similar to that of a brother by marrying one's sister or by being the brother of the person one marries. A *cuñada* (sister-in-law) is like a sister because she is either married to one's brother or is the female sibling of one's spouse.

In similar fashion, a *yerna* (the term used in Moho for daughter-in-law, rather than the more general term, *nuera*) acquires a status that resembles that of a daughter, but the use of a separate term specifies that it is a position held only by reason of matrimony. The same is the case with a *yerno* (son-in-law).

A contrastive analysis of Aymara and Spanish affinal terms reveals the following. There are three features that are essential for distinguishing the relationships created by marriage in the Aymara system. The first of these is the sex of the linking relative. Whereas in Spanish a wife's brother and a husband's brother are both cuñado, in Aymara the spouse's sex makes a significant difference. The second feature is whether the linking relative is blood kin or an affine—in other words, whether the referent is blood kin to one's spouse or the spouse of one's blood kin. In Spanish, there is no terminological distinction between a husband's sister and a brother's wife—both are cuñada or "sister-in-law." In Aymara, however, these form the separate categories ipala and yuqch'a. Finally, in Aymara, the sex of the referent is considered in the primary application of the categories. Yuqch'a and ipala are always females, and tullqa and lari are always males. Although sex becomes irrelevant when the term is subsequently extended to other relatives, the key referent is sex-specific. In Spanish, the sex of the referent is one of the two relevant distinctions, with yerna and cuñada being female and yerno and cuñado being male. The remaining feature that distinguishes Spanish terms is the generation of the referent.

It is obvious that in the Spanish system the major emphasis is not on the categorization of affines but on the establishment of affines as a separate group with different rights and obligations from consanguineal kin. This differs sharply from the Aymara system, where it is the relationship as a giver or taker of a productive member to the parent household that is distinguished. In fact, in the Aymara system, once the relationship and concomitant responsibilities are established as that of a yuqch'a or tullqa, or of a lari or ipala, the distinction between blood kin and affines dissolves with the extension of the terms to the associated consanguineal kin.

At this point it is possible to summarize more succinctly the appropriate definitions of Aymara affinal categories based on the analysis of their distinguishing features. A yuqch'a is a woman who marries a man who is ego's blood relative. A tullqa is a man who marries a woman who is ego's blood relative. A lari is a man who is ego's wife's blood relative. An ipala is a woman who is ego's husband's blood relative. The Aymara terms for the female consanguine of a wife or the male consanguine of a husband are no longer in use in Moho. These categories are referred to by Spanish terms that will be described shortly. In Spanish, yerna and yerno refer to spouses of children, female and male, respectively, while cuñada and cuñado may denote either spouses of siblings or siblings of spouses, with cuñada referring to a female and cuñado to a male. An analysis of these relationships is presented in Figure 2.

THE TRANSLATION TRADITIONS

From the preceding descriptions it should be obvious that the Spanish vocabulary for affinal relatives is not equipped to express the distinctions relevant to Aymara social structure. This, of course, is not to say that the Spanish system is poorly differentiated, any more than it is to say the Aymara system is confusing. The categories that are meaningful in the two languages are the result of two different cultural and historical processes.

The unavoidable fact, however, is that while Spanish is not the first language of the majority of Peruvians, it is the language of the dominant classes in that nation. Native speakers of Aymara and Quechua have increasingly found it necessary to learn Spanish to

Figure 2. Analysis of Affinal Kin Terms in Aymara and Spanish

AYMARA TERMS	through male linking relative	through female linking relative	through relative related by blood	through relative related by marriage	is male	is female
Yuqch'a	+		+			+
Ipala	+			+		+
Tiwula	+			+	+	
Tullqa		+	+		+	
Lari		+		+	+	
Tiyala		+		+		+

SPANISH TERMS	ego's generation	−1 generation	is male	is female
Yerno		+	+	
Yerna (nuera)		+		+
Cuñada	+			+
Cuñado	+		+	

pursue their economic, social, and educational goals for upward mobility. The adoption of the Spanish language, in certain contexts and for certain purposes, however, does not imply an acceptance or adoption of Spanish cultural categories. In cases where Spanish grammar or vocabulary does not conveniently express Aymara conceptions of the world, it may be used creatively to do so. Hardman-de-Bautista (1978:129) has described the manner in which translation equivalences arise in the speech of bilinguals and eventually become translation traditions for expressing the concepts of one culture in the language of another. This process has occurred with the application of Spanish affinal kin terms to Aymara categories.

If Spanish kin terms were applied according to coastal Spanish rules to Aymara affines, both yuqch'a, in the sense of brother's wife, and ipala would be rendered as cuñada. This equation of the two terms obscures the fact that they play two very different roles in a reciprocal relationship with different sorts of duties toward one another. In turn, yuqch'a, or brother's wife, would be called *cuñada*, while yuqch'a, or son's wife, would be referred to as yerna, based on their generational difference. This is despite the fact that they are structurally equivalent in Aymara, which ignores the generational aspect. The use of Spanish terms in such a way would wreak havoc with attempts to speak clearly about Aymara social and economic relationships.

For this reason, the terminological applications represented in Figure 3 were adopted at some point in the past as a convenient way to express the obligation and respect inherent in Aymara social categories when these are discussed in Spanish. In current usage, the Aymara category of lari (wife's brother) is not rendered into Spanish as cuñado (brother-in-law) but as brother (*hermano*). The Aymara of Moho apparently no longer have a native term for wife's sister, who may be referred to as *tiyala*, an Aymarization of the Spanish *tía* (aunt) or at times simply as *hermana* (sister). These terms are conceived of by the Aymara as drawing the referent closer into the kinship circle and as expressing respect and affection. In a related way, one's ipala (husband's sister) is not called by the Spanish term for sister-in-law but by that for a sister. One's husband's brother is referred to as *tiwula*, from the Spanish term for uncle (*tío*), or as hermano (brother). Tullqa and yuqch'a, however, are treated in a very different way. Tullqa is equated with the Spanish category of cuñado (brother-in-law) if he is sister's husband, or yerno (son-in-law) if he is daughter's husband, although, as would be expected, at times there is inadvertent confusion with regard to the generation. Monolingual Aymara speakers, when speaking with people whose native language is Spanish, will often use the translation traditions for affinal kin. In this case, tullqa is most often glossed as yerno for both daughter's husband and sister's husband. Yuqch'a is also equated with the Spanish terms cuñada and yerna. In contrast to the -1 generation gloss term for tullqa, yuqch'a is almost always translated by monolinguals as cuñada (sister-in-law).

The use of brother/sister or aunt/uncle terminology for wife- and husband-givers (lari and ipala) and of in-law terms for the wife- and husband-takers (yuqch'a and tullqa) bears a clear meaning with regard to the Aymara social system. In Aymara, *wali munañaniwa* literally means "We all will love or want him, her, or them very much." When one asks for a translation of the phrase, however, the response is almost inevitably "*Tiene mucho poder*" (He or she is very powerful). The equation of being loved or respected by many people and having power has been noted by other observers in the Andes. (See Isbell 1974.) This forms the basis for the application of more intimate kin terms to those affines to whom one owes more respect.

Those from whom respect is due, in turn, are distanced by the

Figure 3. Translation Traditions—Aymara/Spanish

Lari (wi–bro)	⟶	hermano (brother)
Ipala (hu–si)	⟶	hermana (sister)
Tiyala (wi–si)	⟶	tía (aunt)
Tiwula (hu–bro)	⟶	tío (uncle)
Tullqa (da–hu)	⟶	yerno (son-in-law)
(si–hu)	⟶	cuñado (brother-in-law)—for bilingual speakers
		yerno (son-in-law)—for monolingual speakers
Yuqch'a (so–wi)	⟶	yerna (daughter-in-law)—for bilingual speakers
		cuñada (sister-in-law)—for monolingual speakers
(bro–wi)	⟶	cuñada (sister-in-law)

use of Spanish in-law terms, which are conceived of as less intimate. The Spanish terms are correctly perceived as signifying "one who is not a blood relation"—an outsider. "Outsider" is precisely the connotation given by Isbell (1978), Mayer (1977), Webster (1977), and others to the tullqa/yuqch'a categories, and accurately describes their structural position with regard to their spouse's family as the term is used in Moho.

The way in which translation traditions are used reinforces the behavioral and social structural categories of the Aymara affinal system. Relationships that have organized exchanges of labor and goods between intermarried households continue to play their role in Aymara culture, despite the fact that these relationships are increasingly referred to by Spanish names. There is evidence that a similar process has been at work in the application of Spanish terms to consanguineal kin, but analysis of this issue is beyond the scope of the present paper.

The utility of the way these terms are translated, however, is not always recognized. Many people, hearing a husband's sister referred to as a sister, or a son's wife as a sister-in-law, conclude that the speaker is acting on insufficient knowledge of the Spanish system. Bilinguals, even though they understand and use the translation traditions, may classify them to an outsider as wrong or mistaken. Speakers of coastal Spanish, who understand nothing of the way the terms are used, may attribute such usage to illiteracy or, even worse, to some incapacity to distinguish complex categories on the part of highland speakers.

We have seen, however, that Spanish affinal terms, far from being employed randomly or wrongly, are systematically used to express a part of the Aymara cultural system. The association of those people who provide one with a spouse (ipala, lari) with terms of affection and respect, and to whom one gives up a relation to be their spouse (tullqa, yuqch'a) with terms of greater distance, is not only a carefully ordered use of language; it is a creative manipulation of it.

The implication of this example for other bilingual settings is a simple but important one. We know that errors made by the learners of a new language are not random but are patterned by their native language (Haugen 1956). We should realize also that in social settings where the language of a dominant class is imposed on another sociolinguistic group, what on the surface appear to be errors may really be ordered and imaginative attempts to preserve important aspects of that group's culture.

NOTE

The fieldwork on which this paper was based was funded by an Inter-American Foundation Learning Fellowship for Social Change and was carried out from December 1979 to December 1980 in Moho, Puno, Peru. Institutional affiliation was provided by the Universidad Nacional Técnica del Altiplano.

Aymara and Spanish in Southern Peru: The Relationship of Language to Economic Class and Social Identity

MICHAEL PAINTER

The district of Moho, department of Puno, Peru, is an area in which Spanish, the dominant national language of Peru, and Aymara, a Native American language of the region, coexist. The two languages share a complex interrelationship with the social and economic structure of the district. This paper describes some of the ways that language—more specifically bilingualism—is significant in the social and economic life of Moho.

THE SOCIAL SCIENTIST AND SOCIAL IDENTITY

Questions regarding the relationship between economic class and social or ethnic identity have been of major interest to investigators working in the Andean region in recent years. In describing social stratification, the tradition in Andean anthropology has been to distinguish among three social groups, which are generally termed whites, mestizos, and Indians or peasants. Numerous variations upon this theme exist, but they are generally less than profound. Sometimes a fourth category, cholo, also has been included. This category refers to members of the Native American population who are experiencing upward economic mobility. It represents an attempt to deal with the phenomenon of capitalist penetration into noncapitalist (traditional subsistence farming) areas and the subsequent breakdown of obstacles that previously inhibited upward economic mobility. The cholo, as usually defined in anthropological literature, is socially anomalous because the routes toward economic mobility also may lead away from facile categorizations of people within the tripartite framework mentioned above.

With the increasing penetration of capitalism, the number of socially anomalous people has grown, making the tripartite framework less useful with the passage of time. In fact, one can argue that such a model of social stratification in the Andes has been unsatisfactory throughout the history of its use. Social scientists have not always clearly defined how they apply such terms as whites, mestizos, or Indians. One is left unsure if the terms are being used as labels of social categories that are recognized by the members of a particular society, or if, in fact, they are serving as labels of categories decided upon by the social scientists. The term cholo, for example, is an affectionate term in some areas of the Andes and a pejorative one in others. However, one would be hard pressed to find any area where a structural analysis of its use revealed the term cholo functioning primarily as a label for people who are upwardly mobile. Therefore, it plays a more significant role in the lexicons of Andean scholars than in those of the people. Such inexactitude is indicative of a lack of rigor in either discerning social categories or in applying appropriate labels to them.

This lack of rigor may be attributed to a number of factors, two of which are directly related to bilingualism. The coexistence of Spanish with a Native American language is a basic, though often unstated, characteristic of many Andean societies that may have profound implications for social structure. Unfortunately, many investigators have gone to the field unprepared to deal with bilingualism in carrying out their research. More frequently than not, researchers have carried out their investigations only in Spanish, the dominant language of the region. It is therefore impossible to empirically verify the discriminations of social categories made by non-Spanish speakers and to determine the variability of occurrence of the discriminations within the population. Social scientists who must work only in Spanish must base their analyses upon what they are able to observe directly and what Spanish-speaking interpreters have told them. This automatically precludes any comparisons being made among the perceptions of social stratification by different groups within a population, and obscures any distinction between the observations of the analyzer and the analyzed.

The confusion associated with the question of whether the social discriminations made among groups within an Andean society are based upon class or ethnicity is a second factor related to the question of bilingualism. An investigator who gathers data in the manner described above is not in a position to know if the discriminations made among groups in a society belong to the domain of class, of ethnicity, or of something else altogether. This lack of precision was not as apparent when capitalist penetration into many of the areas studied was less extensive. Before capitalism became the dominant mode of production in the countryside, there was often a strong positive correlation between a social structure based upon ethnicity with whites at the top and Indians at the bottom and an economic class structure characterized by unequal distribution of wealth along similar lines. However, capitalist penetration is typically initiated and directed by groups outside the local Andean society, and its entrance into an area may weaken or break the hold of dominant social groups upon economic opportunity. When this occurs, the positive correlation between a social hierarchy based upon ethnic identity and economic class is also weakened or broken down. The result is that people on the bottom of the social hierarchy may suddenly appear at the top of the economic hierarchy. Socially oppressed peasants or Indians may control more wealth than many members of the groups that have oppressed them, and, more significantly from the perspective of a class analysis, they may employ other peasants or Indians as wage laborers for the purpose of extracting a surplus.

LANGUAGE, SOCIAL IDENTITY, AND ECONOMIC CLASS IN MOHO

Language often serves as an important marker of the boundaries among social groups, although the precise way in which language fills this role naturally will vary over time. This paper examines the relationship of language to social identity and economic class in

Moho, an Aymara-speaking district of Puno department, Peru. Through an analysis of their distinguishing features, the social categories that divide the population of Moho are elucidated and the features upon which social discriminations are based are examined. This approach is based upon the methodologies delineated by Lounsbury (1964) and Goodenough (1965). Miracle (1976) has demonstrated the utility of formal analysis as a tool for examining Aymara social relations.

The district of Moho is located on the northeastern shore of Lake Titicaca on the Peruvian altiplano. It ranges in elevation from approximately 3,812 meters above sea level along the shore of Lake Titicaca to approximately 4,200 meters above sea level in the northeastern corner, where it approaches the eastern range of the Andes. From the lower to higher elevations, a land-use pattern of intensive agriculture gives way to a mixed pattern of agriculture and livestock, which in turn gives way to highly dispersed herding communities. Cash-generating activities revolve around the cultivation of coffee and citrus fruits in the Tambopata Valley on the eastern slopes of the Andes, smuggling, and seasonal migration to the cities in search of wage labor.

Moho is not the conflict-ridden society that has been described for other areas of the Andes, where being associated with one group or faction automatically makes one an enemy of other groups or factions. In spite of very deep divisions, a united front is presented to outsiders. This image of unity is strengthened by the fact that nearly everyone speaks Aymara. The only people who do not are those, such as police and school officials, who have come to Moho from other areas. It is difficult to find signs of any stigma attached to Aymara or to elicit any sort of negative response when talking about the language. The use of Aymara is so general that outsiders are often put under considerable pressure to learn it. There are a number of families, particularly in the town, who do forbid their children to speak Aymara at home. However, this ostensibly does not reflect negative feelings about Aymara as much as a fear that children will lack the necessary control of Spanish to do well in school.

What does have a stigma attached to it is monolingualism. Monolinguals are referred to as being lazy and lifeless and are frequently the butts of bilingual jokes. This refers to monolingual Spanish speakers as well as to monolingual Aymara speakers. A man from another region of Peru who married a woman from Moho and lived there for forty years without learning Aymara was constantly held up as a negative example. The fact that he was from a Quechua-speaking area but could speak no Quechua made matters even worse, as most moheños know at least the greetings and courtesy phrases of Cuzco Quechua. Attitudes regarding language are closely inter-related with social divisions in Moho. However, as this description indicates, the relationship is much more complex than a simple cor-relation of Spanish being associated with certain groups and Ay-mara with others.

As noted, there are profound social divisions in Moho society. I first learned of them through accounts of local and regional history. Provincial and departmental monographs refer to an uprising or re-bellion on the part of Indians that reached a peak of violence in late 1923. These accounts are similar to those of local elites in Moho, who tell stories of how the Indians marched on the town, forcing women and children to seek refuge in the church and the men to make an armed defense of their families. Those in the rural areas recall attacks made on their communities by armed townspeople in which rural inhabitants were killed or tortured, livestock stolen, and crops destroyed.

This conflict between the local elites and the socially defined In-dian or peasant population was the culmination of several years of agitation on the part of Indians to put an end to labor obligations and such petty abuses as dress proscriptions. It was most certainly, however, in favor of the establishment of schools in the rural com-munities. In their efforts to obtain schools, the Indians received support from the Seventh-Day Adventist Church and the Lima-based Sociedad pro Derecha Indígena, also known as the Tawantinsuyo Society.

This was viewed as subversive by the local elites, and, when the Indians began performing military exercises and mobilizing around the towns, the elite panicked. In the area of the provincial capital of Huancané, troops from Puno were brought in to suppress the Indians, which they did with a vengeance, reportedly killing hundreds (Hazen 1974). No present-day informants in Moho, among either the town elites or the rural inhabitants, could cite any specific acts of violence the Indians were supposed to have committed. However, the townspeople launched a series of preemptive assaults on rural communities, killing large numbers and committing acts of indiscriminate torture. The rampage of the townspeople was stopped only when some Indians managed to escape to Lima and make a report to President Leguía, who brought the violence under control by dispatching troops from the capital. This period is still very much a part of the collective memory, including the roles that particular families and individuals played in the course of events.

Today, incidents of violence are exceedingly rare. Social divisions are marked by asymmetries in interpersonal behavior. Some people consistently fail to greet certain individuals on the street, for example, or they will call someone by name without employing courtesy titles such as *tata* or *mama* and señor or señora. (See Briggs 1976.) Labels are applied to people, either by others or by themselves, to distinguish individuals as members of social groups. In the town, for example, one might hear people being referred to as *vecinos* (town elites) and *indios* (Indians).[1] In the countryside, people refer to themselves and other rural dwellers as *campesinos* (peasants) and *jaqi* (human beings), while townspeople are known as *misti*. The potential depth of this division is clearly implied by contrasting misti with human beings. Human and nonhuman are contrasting inflectional categories in Aymara, so that a speaker is obligated to specify whether what is being talked about is human or nonhuman. Any hint that a person is somehow not human is one of the gravest insults an Aymara speaker can produce (Hardman-de-Bautista 1978).

Formal analysis was employed in order to define the social categories to which these labels are applied. Native discourse on social structure was analyzed to determine the characteristics associated by the population with different social groups. Follow-up questions were prepared to permit further analysis of frequently repeated themes. These follow-up questions were designed to elicit definitions of the behaviors associated with social groups, and to encourage people to state explicitly the assumptions and values that cause them to view these behaviors as positive or negative.

People in Moho customarily discriminate social categories on the

Figure 1. Social strata as labeled by people of Moho

Features	Campesino	Misti	Domain
Works own fields	+	+	
Sells labor	+	+	
Hires labor[1]		+	
Exchanges labor	+	+	
Has maid		+	Work
Children herd	+	+	
Walks to border[2]	+		
Owns land in Tambopata[3]	+	+	
Makes own poncho	+	+	
Adventist	+	+	
Catholic	+	+	Religion
Sunday Mass—morning	+		
Sunday Mass—evening		+	
Speaks Spanish	+	+	Language
Speaks Aymara	+	+	
Lives in town		+	
Lives in community	+		
Carnival—campo dance group	+	+	Residence
Carnival—town dance group		+	
Celebrates campo fiestas	+	+	
Celebrates town fiestas[4]		+	
Wears ojotas or goes barefoot	+	+	
Wears shoes	+	+	Dress
Wears pollera skirt (women)	+	+	
Family members killed in 1923	+	+	
Family members attacked			
communities in 1923		+	
Greets all people he/she knows	+	+	
Does not greet everyone		+	Human/nonhuman
Shares food	+	+	
Eats hot lunch (almuerzo)		+	Food
Eats cold lunch (fiambres)	+	+	
Spanish surname	+	+	Names
Elite surname		+	

See notes on facing page.

basis of a simple opposition: the group to which they belong, and everyone else. They initially responded to queries by describing the group to which they did not belong in stereotyped pejorative terms. For example, rural dwellers customarily refer to town elites as being lazy, while the latter view rural dwellers as overly ambitious (*ambiciosos*). Further elicitation revealed a list of behaviors pertaining to the domain of work, for which the customarily used pejoratives serve as cover terms. The distinguishing behavioral features thus obtained are illustrated in Figure 1. These features are not the spontaneous distinctions made by people in the course of their daily lives, but are the result of further elicitation regarding those distinctions. It is interesting that while rural dwellers and townspeople have distinct pejoratives that they employ to refer to one another, the behavioral correlates to which the respective pejoratives refer are the same for both groups.

However, Figure 1 illustrates that the behavioral features elicited in the manner described do not distinguish two social categories on the basis of an us versus them opposition. This indicates that, if the distinguishing features were correctly elicited, an unstated or unmarked social category must exist in addition to the other two.

This third, unmarked category (Figure 2), which will be referred to as the town Aymara in this paper, shares some features with the campesinos and some with the vecinos. At the same time, the town Aymara are different from the other two groups. They are not campesinos because they live in the town and not the country, and they are not vecinos because they do not share elite family names.

Figure 2 illustrates five features in three domains that are shared by all social strata. Yet they repeatedly were mentioned by people during elicitation sessions that dealt with social stratification. The reasons for this warrant some discussion. Figures 1 and 2 show that members of all social strata are Catholic. This is true because at

---

[1] Refers to *mink'a*, which in Moho designates the sale of one's labor for money. A campesino may pay workers; however, it is the right of the worker to decide whether to exchange labor for labor or labor for money. Misti may offer no choice.

[2] Refers to the willingness to walk long distances without transport. The border with Bolivia often was cited as a place campesinos walk to trade but misti do not.

[3] Coffee growing region in Tambopata Valley, Sandia Province, Puno department.

[4] Campo fiestas include Candelaria, San Juan, and Santa Rosa de Lima. Town fiestas include Santa Cruz and Exaltación de la Cruz.

Figure 2. Social strata as distinguished by elicited features

Features	Campesino	Town Aymara	Vecino	Domain
Works own fields	+	+		
Sells labor	+	+		
Hires labor		+	+	
Exchanges labor	+	+		
Has maid			+	Work
Children herd	+	+		
Walks to border	+			
Owns land in Tambopata	+	+		
Makes own poncho	+	+		
Adventist	+	+		
Catholic	+	+	+	Religion
Sunday Mass—morning	+			
Sunday Mass—evening		+	+	
Speaks Spanish	+	+	+	Language
Speaks Aymara	+	+	+	
Lives in town		+	+	
Lives in community	+			
Carnival—campo dance group	+	+		Residence
Carnival—town dance group		+	+	
Celebrates campo fiestas	+	+		
Celebrates town fiestas		+	+	
Wears ojotas or goes barefoot	+	+		
Wears shoes	+	+	+	Dress
Wears pollera skirt (women)	+	+	+	
Family members killed in 1923	+	+		
Family members attacked communities in 1923			+	
Greets all people he/she knows	+	+		Human/
Does not greet everyone			+	nonhuman
Shares food	+	+		
Eats hot lunch (almuerzo)		+	+	Food
Eats cold lunch (fiambres)	+	+		
Spanish surname	+	+	+	Names
Elite surname			+	

least nominal Catholicism was obligatory until recently. What is important in the domain of religion is that the vecinos have not adopted Adventism, and that the town Aymara and vecinos do not attend Mass at the same time as campesinos who are Catholic.

Today, objectively definable clothing differences corresponding to social strata are minimal. In fact, the only obvious difference is that vecinos will never wear *ojotas* (rubber tire sandals) or go bare-footed. People from all social strata may be observed wearing shoes. Likewise, women from all social strata may be seen wearing the full-cut *polleras* (skirts) and derbies. It will be recalled, however, that one of the reasons for the 1923 civil disturbances was to end the requirement that they wear Indian dress. This forbade the rural people from wearing shoes, and limited clothing to items of home-spun wool (*bayeta*). Men wore knee-length pants and a tunic-style shirt, and women wore polleras and woolen blouses. Vecino men wore the Western-style of the period, while the women wore pol-leras, although of finer fabrics than homespun wool.

Today, one rarely sees campesino men wearing the short pants, although they frequently wear homespun clothing while working in the fields. For conducting business in town or attending a celebra-tion, they frequently will wear clothing as stylish as that of any vecino. Campesino women customarily wear homespun polleras for fieldwork and others of finer materials for going to town or special occasions. There are also campesino women who wear slacks or Western-style skirts. Vecino women will either wear polleras, though not of bayeta, or Western skirts or slacks.

Clothing bears an interesting relationship to social identity for two reasons. First, it is of interest that vecino women wear polleras. The pollera is a Spanish imposition that was intended as a visual marker of Indian social status. The facts that vecino women have worn them for a long time and that there are many who continue to wear them today suggest that ranks of the vecino social stratum are not and have not been closed to people entering from the other social strata. In the neighboring district of Vilquechico, Galdo Pa-gaza (1962) noted that women born of the town elite frequently married outsiders. The men frequently married women of families with lower social status. A similar pattern exists in Moho.

Second, although the 1923 conflict was a turning point of sorts in the treatment of Indians, dress proscriptions and other labels of subserviency did not disappear immediately. The vecinos were at least as passionate about maintaining this symbol of their superiority as were the campesinos about abolishing it. Although there are no active restrictions on how campesinos dress today, vecinos still enjoy making snide remarks about people whose clothes are considered too nice for their station in life. Thus clothing remains an active marker of social identity.

The speaking of Spanish or Aymara is also a feature that does not distinguish anything today. However, like clothing, this too is closely associated with the violence of 1923, and is also an issue with tremendous emotional impact. Currently, most vecinos are bilingual in Spanish and Aymara, although there are monolingual Aymara speakers among older women. Perhaps half of the people in the countryside are bilingual, with their proficiency in Spanish varying from complete fluency to very poor control. Through the school system, increasing numbers of children in the countryside are becoming proficient in Spanish.

In the past, particularly before 1923, there were active prohibitions against the use of Spanish by people from the countryside. There were always, of course, some people who learned the language, but informants recall that people who made the mistake of allowing a vecino to hear them use Spanish were likely to be beaten or even killed. Spanish was a monopoly that the vecinos used to maintain other monopolies such as access to the legal system or economic opportunity.

One of the acts of insurrection that led to the violence of 1923 was the establishment of schools in their communities for the purpose of learning to speak, read, and write Spanish. The building of these schools was carried out with the aid of the Seventh-Day Adventist Church in some cases and the Lima-based Tawantinsuyo Society in others. In the neighboring district of Huancané, some communities went so far as to establish a new town called Wancho-Lima. They sent representatives to meet with President Leguía, who is said to have given them a charter for their town and a map of Lima to use as a guide for constructing it. The town was built with the streets laid out to correspond to the arrangement of streets in central Lima. Within its limits, it was prohibited to speak any language other than Spanish (Gallegos n.d.).

From modern accounts, it seems that the building of schools more than any other single factor provoked the vecinos to violence. On the part of the rural dwellers, knowing Spanish was the key to satisfying their rising aspirations for a better standard of living, while for the vecinos, it was equally as much the key for maintaining their dominant position. The right to speak Spanish and to learn to read and write it was won only at the cost of the lives of many people from the countryside. It is small wonder that the initial implementation of a bilingual education program in some schools by the Peruvian Ministry of Education in 1980 was greeted with extreme suspicion rather than optimism by campesinos in Moho.

The presence of monolingual Aymara speakers among the vecino women, like the wearing of polleras, is an indication of upward social mobility that brought them into the ranks of the elite families. Also, as in the issue of clothing, it is difficult to objectively define current social divisions on the basis of language. However, such divisions did exist in the not so distant past, and the association of language with social status remains in the minds of people even though it is difficult to observe its role in current social interactions.

The final feature providing no contrast in the current social context of Moho is the distribution of Spanish surnames. This too may be explained historically, but not by the violence of 1923. Spanish family names became widespread over the countryside soon after the Conquest, when many people adopted them for the purpose of baptism. The spread of Spanish surnames was facilitated by the tremendous population decline following the Conquest and by the forced resettlement of those who survived to form the town of Moho. In later years, many people found it to their advantage to adopt Spanish surnames along with other trappings of Spanish culture. It seems that the surnames function as a metonym for Spanish values, although their actual distribution bears no relation to the social identity of the people who have them.

As has been stressed, the categories that have been defined here—those of campesino, town Aymara, and vecino—are not ethnosemantic. They do not correspond to customary local perceptions of social structure, but are the product of a formal analysis of features derived from elicited responses by informants regarding the different social groups to be found in the district. Although an abstraction of local perceptions, the validity of the categories may be ascertained through direct observation of the asymmetrical interactions that occur between individuals of different social strata. Such interactions are summarized in Figure 3. Interactions between individuals in the respective social categories are listed in the left-hand column. Particular kinds of interactions appear at the top of the figure. The first five interactions are related to the distinctive features listed in Figures 1 and 2. The other two (*compadrazgo* [godparenthood] and marriage) were not included as distinctive features, but are important social bonds formed among the different groups.

The social categories described for Moho may appear to resemble the tripartite descriptions criticized at the beginning of this paper. There are, however, two important differences. First, an explicit and formal methodology was employed both in the collection of data and in their manipulation for the purpose of deriving the social categories and delineating their parameters. Such an approach allows the social discriminations made by the local population to be distinguished from those made by the investigator as a result of analysis, because research in the native language or languages of informants is a basic assumption and because the step of converting

Figure 3. Interactions between members of different social strata

	greets	asks to work	shares food	dance together	invite to house	compa-drazgo	marriage
campesino→campesino	+	+	+	+	+	+	+
campesino→town Aymara	+		+	+	+	+	+
campesino→vecino	+		+			+	
town Aymara→campesino	+	+	+	+		+	+
town Aymara→town Aymara	+	+	+	+	+	+	+
town Aymara→vecino	+		+		+	+	+
vecino→campesino		+					
vecino→town Aymara	+	+					+
vecino→vecino	+		+	+	+	+	+

ethnosemantic data to distinguishing features is an explicit inductive step.

Second, the features upon which the discriminations are based are social and not economic in nature. Other descriptions of social stratification in Puno (Bourricaud 1967), as well as in other areas of Peru, have discussed social stratification as part and parcel of economic class, making no distinction between one's economic class and social status. In fact, social categories do have economic implications. Vecinos tend to be professionals, for example, while jobs involving manual labor or commerce are dominated by people in the other categories. Bonds of compadrazgo or marriage are formed with the purpose of increasing the economic security of family units. However, wealth was never mentioned by informants as a characteristic of a particular social status. At one time, this probably would not have been the case since vecinos controlled access to economic wealth. It was undoubtedly for this reason that Bourricaud (1967) and others found it convenient to discuss economic class and social or ethnic identity together.

However, the changes Bourricaud observed occurring in the city of Puno in the early 1950s, which prompted him to discuss at length the differences among cholos, Indians, and mestizos and to attempt to analyze who was more Indian and why, were symptomatic of the breakdown between economic class and social status. In Moho, groups other than the vecinos have been very successful in taking advantage of economic opportunities. Indeed, the names of vecino families never came up in discussions of the wealthiest families of the district. The acquisition of wealth by members of the campesino and town Aymara social strata has led to the emergence of class differentiations characteristic of capitalist society within each group. Campesinos and town Aymara are involved in such positions as wage laborers, independent mercantilists, and the employers of large numbers of workers. These activities bring people of similar social status into diverse relationships with land, labor, and capital.

CONCLUSIONS

This paper describes aspects of social or ethnic identity and their relationship to economic class in a bilingual setting. In such a setting, the role of language is complex and frequently ambiguous. Because a positive correlation between economic class and social identity can no longer be assumed for Andean society, it is argued that the relationship between the two must be made explicit and dealt with on the basis of the particulars of the case under study. Formal analysis is suggested as a means of doing this. This approach reveals that, although the local population sees only two social categories, the features cited as being distinctive mark three social categories. In addition, the case of Moho indicates that when formal analysis is applied to social and economic questions, particularly in areas undergoing rapid change, the interpretation of results may require an historical approach. Clothing and language differences provide examples of how markers of social boundaries may change more slowly in the minds of people than they do in observable behavior. The existence of such a mental lag plays an important role in understanding the relationship of language to the broader spectrum of social interaction.

Current language attitudes are the result of particular and relatively recent historical processes. Spanish was perceived as a key to increased economic opportunity for the people who did not belong to the vecino group, and the efforts by vecinos to preserve their monopoly of Spanish in the face of the social unrest of 1923 served as confirmation of that perception. People in the countryside died for it, and continue to guard their right to learn Spanish because of its relationship to economic opportunity. Aymara, on the other hand, is the language of homeland and family for people of all social groups. For the vecinos, the significance of Aymara is increasingly confined to this folkloric sentimentality because being bilingual no longer has the economic advantages for them that it held when people in the countryside were monolingual.

For the campesinos and the town Aymara, it is being Aymara and having that language as their own that makes them different. It is being and speaking Aymara that makes them more polite than the vecinos, and they relate it to their identity as people who were willing to risk their lives for education, which, of course, included learning Spanish. In addition, there are increasingly economic advantages to be had from speaking Aymara. There are now a number of people who are socially campesinos or town Aymara who are wealthy enough to have considerable economic and political power at the departmental and regional level. Like the vecinos, they tend to dispense the largesse of their positions to people with origins similar to their own. For this reason, Moho is different from areas where bilingualism has meant the slow replacement of a Native American language by Spanish; rather, bilingualism may be seen as symptomatic of the vitality of Aymara.

NOTES

This paper is based upon research sponsored by a Learning Fellowship for Social Change from the Inter-American Foundation and a Fulbright-Hays Fellowship for Doctoral Research, which was carried out in the district of Moho, Puno department, Peru, in 1979–80. I should like to thank Juan Lira Condori and Yolanda López Callo for their able assistance while I was conducting research in their home district. Jane Collins, M. J. Hardman-de-Bautista, and Anthony Oliver-Smith read an earlier version of this paper and provided numerous useful comments.
1. Although Indian is a literal gloss for the Spanish term indio, the English usage does not carry the pejorative connotation of the Spanish.

Diglossia, Regionalism, and National Language Policy: A Comparison of Spain and the Philippines

GABRIEL DECICCO AND JOEL M. MARING

There seem to be three minimal requirements for recognition as a nation: a flag, an anthem, and a national language. The first two seldom pose a problem. Language is of another dimension. Regionalism, political dominance of one group over another, competing literary standards, media preference, religion, arbitrary boundaries, and even location of the capital—all contribute to the selection of a national language. Enormous stress, even violence, may result from attempts to resolve issues of national language and language policy.

If the problem is characteristically associated with recently formed states, it is by no means limited to them. The birth of modern nations such as the Philippines came after World War II, but Spain achieved its present shape almost five hundred years ago. In fact, there are few countries today that do not have two or more indigenous, immigrant, or colonial languages competing for equal or superior status. Problems related to language selection are numerous, for all too frequently the issue merely reflects deeper differences. Among newly formed states, there may be a choice between perpetuating a colonial language of international use, and simultaneously neutralizing regional jealousies and giving national status to a vernacular language, which symbolizes the pride of nationhood and the equality of status of the noncolonial culture with that of other nations. For both newly formed and older countries, the recognition of regional cultures contributes to regional pride and integrity, but it may also open the door to conflicts over regional dominance at the national level.

The issue of the arbitrariness of a nation's political boundaries is often significant. The colonial cutting up of the world's territorial pie has left ethnic groups straddling political boundaries. But even among older nations, these lines have fluctuated through conquest and political assimilation.

The existence of situations of diglossia—that is, the recognition of both formal literary and colloquial standards of language—also poses problems for new nations with competing standards and older nations where regional groups seek autonomous recognition.[1]

SPAIN

Spain has an especially acute language problem. Within its borders are four indigenous languages: Castilian, the country's official national language; Catalan, an official language of Andorra, closely related to Provençal; Galician, a Portuguese dialect; and Basque. While the first three are Romance languages, Basque is a renowned isolate among Indo-European languages spoken on both sides of the Spanish/French border.[2] Many Basque speakers reside within the boundaries of the former kingdom of Navarre, which was incorporated into Aragon in 1517. Catalonia became a part of Aragon in the fifteenth century—although it reverted to French control on several occasions. Galicia was the Spanish enclave from which the Christian reconquest of the country began. Spain's boundaries were more or less set, then, by the end of the fifteenth century, although many regions retained a degree of ethnic integrity and their own language.

As recently as December 24, 1980, the newspaper *Correo de Andalucía* headlined its report of a meeting of the Council of Ministers with "A law will regulate the use of the flag, the language and the significance of the word 'national.'" The context of the headline is the autonomy recently granted various regions. Since the advent of a democratic form of government in 1975, the drive for autonomy has been strong in many regions. They have, in fact, designed their flags and written their anthems; several already had a language. The latter is unquestionably the most important, for it has long been recognized that language is a unifying force among ethnic groups and a potential rallying factor for separatism in multilingual states. It is not surprising, then, that the Franco government restricted the use of regional languages. The decision also was motivated by the fact that the Basque Provinces and Catalonia had been tenacious defenders of the Spanish Republic.

During the Republican period, language policy had been far different. Politically weak, the Republic made every effort to gain support from the various regions, especially the economically powerful Basque country and Catalonia. Laws were passed favoring a federalist rather than centrist form of government. On April 19, 1931, a decree recognized the right, in Catalonia, to teach both kindergarten and primary school classes in "the mother tongue." A subsequent order established departments of Catalan language and literature in the regional teachers' colleges.

Similar permission was granted other regions, but the Catalan case deserves special attention because of the widespread use of the language throughout the region. The majority of Catalans speak their native tongue, and, for many, it is their first language. Even today, after years of restrictions, most Catalans speak Castilian with a Catalan accent—sometimes affected to prove their ethnicity. Furthermore, Catalan is the preference of all social strata, including the regional elite. This is in marked contrast to Basque and Galician, which, according to Múgica Urdangarín (1976), have a high "asphyxiation level." He notes that if there is one monolingual Castilian among twenty-five Basque bilinguals, there is a 63 percent probability that the conversation will be in Castilian. With two Castilians among fifty Basques, the probability of using Castilian rises to 85 percent, while three Castilians among seventy-five Basques guarantee the use of the national language. Native Basques are, incidentally, among the most economically powerful segments in the country and probably control more than half the nation's wealth through banking and industry. Yet, only among the local, rural population is the language preferred. Galician is the language of the regional lower classes, and its asphyxiation level is probably higher than that of Basque. Among Catalans, however, the picture is reversed. Three bilingual Catalans in a reunion with ninety-seven Castilians will probably attempt to conduct the conversation in Catalan. Nevertheless, none of the three languages is in danger of extinction, despite attempts by the Franco government to suppress them.

The language policies of the Nationalist government became clear even before the end of hostilities. Immediately after these regions were occupied, the Statutes of Autonomy granted Catalonia and the Basque Provinces were revoked. The revocation of autonomy included the prohibition to use the regional languages officially. The political climate is evident in the wording of the decree printed in the *Boletín Oficial del Estado*[3] on April 5, 1938, not long after the occupation of Barcelona: " . . . the Statutes of Catalonia, conceded by the Republic in an evil hour, cease to be valid, in the Spanish juridical order, [retroactive] from July 16, 1936." Revocation of the Basque Statutes came after the occupation of Bilbao.

To insure unity, the Nationalists wanted to impose Castilian, and even the Bureau of Vital Statistics came under their scrutiny. On May 21, 1938, a law was promulgated that prohibited " . . . [naming children] with individualized words that express [such] concepts as liberty and democracy or the names of persons who had intervened in the Russian-Jewish Revolution that the dead republic took as a model and archtype . . . [or] . . . abstract or tendentious names." Spanish citizens "inappropriately named" before that date had to have a suitable Castilian name inserted on their certificate. Any inscription found in the civil registry in any language other than Castilian was null and without legal value. This included not only birth but marriage and death records as well. On May 16, 1940, a decree began: "Not through any petty spirit of xenophobia, but because of the exigencies of respect due that which is intrinsically ours . . . such as our language . . . [it is necessary to eliminate] vices of language that, *transcending the partially incoercible environment of private life. . . .*" [Our italics.] Several articles of the law then prohibited foreign words in advertisements, signs, and the like found in bars, hotels, theaters, and all other public places. Eventually the order was extended to commercial labels and, by 1945, to the naming of all types of maritime vessels. There was gradual relaxation in the enforcement of these restrictions as the Nationalist government became confident in its power. Nevertheless, even as late as 1970, some of the laws remained on the books, and prior police permission was required to publish ads or announcements in any language other than Castilian (although this was granted automatically if there was no political content in the subject matter). All foreign languages were included in the prohibitions, but the laws were aimed at Catalan, Basque, and Galician far more than at other non-Spanish languages. This is evident in the subtly worded preamble of April 21, 1964, that canceled most of the restrictions. It began, "Having disappeared, the circumstances that counseled the Ministerial Orders. . . ."

Naturally, all official documents and communications had to be in Castilian. On May 21, 1938, after the occupation of the Basque country, the language policy of the Franco government was made clear. The following is from an order that prohibited the use of any language other than Castilian in titles, minutes of meetings, by-laws, assemblies, and the like.

> Surely, more through the inertia of custom than through the spirit of maintaining sentiments which have certainly disappeared forever, and were stimulated only by an audacious minority that has fled Spain in defeat, some cooperative societies of the Basque provinces still retain their [indigenous] names, or permit the circulation of statutes and regulations edited in the Basque language, even if they are almost always accompanied by translation in Castilian. And it being absolutely necessary that Nationalist and Spanish sentiments manifest themselves without doubt or vacillation of any kind especially in the spirit and in the deed of [official] entities, *a fact that does not deny the respect due the use of dialects in private family relations, after prior notice to the Ministry of the Interior. . . .* [Our italics.]

Requiring a permit to use a regional language in "family relations" was unenforceable, of course, but this gave the government license to step in if a large, extended family reunion was used to cover up a political meeting.

Basque and Catalan bore the brunt of linguistic restrictions, inasmuch as they were "separatist" regions. Franco was Galician and more sympathetic to his own. Besides, Galician is a Portuguese dialect (or vice versa), and it would hardly do to make too strong a prohibition against the language of a strong ally. Treaties with Portugal included the creation of university chairs of Portuguese language and literature and the permission to teach the language in schools. On March 4, 1955, the Rosalía de Castro chair of Galician language, literature, and history was established in the University of Madrid. No such action was taken on behalf of Basque or Catalan.

In Spain, all four indigenous languages are considered Spanish languages, so that the adjective Spanish is seldom used to define only one of them. In most official documents, therefore, the term Castilian is used to refer to that language known elsewhere as Spanish. Nevertheless, during the Franco era, the word Spanish appears often, especially in orders originating from the Ministry of Education. Thus we have examples such as the following: "National Language—The Spanish language, fundamental union of the Hispanic community, will be obligatory and the object of special cultivation, as a necessary instrument of expression and human formation in all national primary schools" (Order of the Ministry of Education dated July 17, 1945).

A relaxation of restrictions placed on regional languages preceded Franco's death. In May 1975, a decree authorized the teaching of "native languages" in schools. Another, issued the same year and entitled *Regional Languages*, begins: "Inspired by the desire to respect and protect regional languages, leaving as a foregone conclusion the transcendental importance of Castilian as the official tongue. . . ." Following this preamble, six articles that set down the new policy can be summarized as follows:

1. Regional languages are the cultural heritage of the Spanish nation and will be protected by the State.
2. Regional languages can be utilized by all means of diffusion.
3. Castilian, the official national language and vehicle of communication for all Spaniards, will be used in all acts of the higher organs of the State.
4. No Spaniard can be the object of discrimination for not knowing or using a regional language.
5. Local entities and corporations can orally use regional languages for internal affairs.
6. Regional languages can be taught in schools.

Beginning in 1978, a number of laws established the rights of each linguistic community to inaugurate bilingual systems of education. According to the preamble of the Decree of June 23, 1978, "Consideration of the linguistic reality of Spain, multiple and varied, imposes the necessity of elaborating legal channels that incorporate into the educational system, the teaching of the distinct languages spoken in Spain." Nevertheless, the Order of September 14, 1978, makes it clear that "The teaching of the Catalan language or the development of school programs in Catalan does not suppose . . . limits on the level of proficiency students must attain in written and oral Castilian, official language of the State."

Decrees published April 20, July 20, August 3, and September 7, 1979, grant equal license to the Basque Provinces, Galicia, Valencia, and the Balearic Islands, respectively. The last two are interesting because they demonstrate the emotional and political content of national and regional language policy. Valencian and Mallorquin are Catalan dialects, but nowhere with regard to Valencia does the decree make mention of Catalan. Rather, the reference is to the Valencian language. In its decree, the term Mallorquin is used frequently, but it is clearly recognized that it is a " . . . style of the Catalan language. . . ."

Recent changes in the languages policies of Spain affect not only the educational system. In a decree issued May 10, 1979, the use of vernaculars is permitted in all local affairs, although it requires that all communications be translated into Castilian. As the preamble of this decree states, "The necessity of guaranteeing an adequate and easy expression and communication of thoughts, ideas, and opinions obligates the realization that there exists, in important parts of the Spanish territory, large sectors of the population that have received, as maternal languages, languages distinct from Castilian."

It becomes evident that political expediency, as much as linguistic reality, dictates national language policy in Spain. Recently held "plebiscites" have resulted in a proliferation of "autonomous regions." Even Andalusia now has its autonomous government—together with its flag and its anthem. It too is determined to have its own language, somewhat puzzling in view of the fact that Castilian is spoken there. Nevertheless, the Andalusians have long been ridiculed by linguistic elitists for the "defective" dialect they now take pride in speaking. In Seville, the Seminar on Andalusian Speech (reported in the newspaper *ABC*, November 6, 1980) concluded that Andalusian was a superior form of Castilian and "the only possibility of survival" for the language—a somewhat pretentious declaration in view of the fact that Castilian is spoken by hundreds of millions throughout the world. Nevertheless, it does point out the importance of the language issue.

THE PHILIPPINES

During four centuries of colonial rule, the Philippines had imposed on it the languages of its rulers, first Spanish and then English. These two languages still play dominant roles, even though a vernacular-based language, Pilipino, has been given national language status. Clearly, the language issues in the Philippines focus on the questions of whether or how long to retain English as a language of education and access to international affairs, how to develop and promote a vernacular-based language as a symbol of nationhood, and how to deal with the intense regionalism and competing vernaculars of the country. President Marcos, in his address to the Conference on the Standardisation of Asian Languages in 1974, called for equal national status of Pilipino and English.

> The future Philippines should be one where the government and the people can communicate in a single medium easily mastered by the masses of the people, a language most identified with the struggles of the nation for independence and dignity, a language that will serve, like the flag itself, as a binding force for permanent national cohesion and solidarity at all levels of society. There is no implication here that we are ready to renounce our possession of English as a world language. For Filipinos in the indefinite future, English will serve as the key to the storehouse of the world's knowledge, and in an age of knowledge explosion, it will be folly to renounce our comparative advantage in our possession of the English language. (Marcos 1978:8.)

As is the case with many nations that have emerged from colonialism in Africa and Asia, the ethnolinguistic base of the Philippines is very complex. The approximately seventy-five Philippine languages, part of the North Indonesian group, belong to the Austronesian language family. While linguistic research has not fully determined the state of their internal genetic relationships, the languages divide into three subgroups: Northern Luzon, with Ilocano the dominant language and including also Ifugao, Bontok, Kalinga; the Central Philippines, including Tagalog, Cebuano, Hiligaynon,

Waray-Waray, and Bicol; and Southern Mindanao, including Tau Sug, Maguindanao, Bilaan, Samal, and Maranao (Maring and Maring 1973:115). While the diversity is great, most languages are represented by small percentages of the population, and eight languages, spoken by over 86 percent of the population, predominate. These are: Cebuano (24 percent), Tagalog (21 percent), Ilocano (12 percent), Hiligaynon (10 percent), Bicol (8 percent), Waray-Waray (6 percent), Pampangan (3 percent), and Pangasinan (2 percent). Cebuano, Hiligaynon, and Waray-Waray are closely related, and are often referred to jointly as Visayan (Bisayan). Both Pilipino (derived from Tagalog) and English, as national languages, are spoken by about 50 percent of the population; Spanish is spoken by only about 3 percent (Maring and Maring 1973:109). The eight major languages are recognized as politically important and, except for the strategic location of the capital in a Tagalog area and promotion of Tagalog by the Japanese, any one might have played a more important role as a basis for a national language. Asuncion-Landé (1971) notes that all of the eight elected presidents have come from these major groups, as have their vice-presidential running mates, although always chosen from different linguistic groups than the president.

The issue of vernacular versus an international language has long existed in the Philippines, having first been a policy concern early in the Spanish colonial period. Ernest J. Frei (1959) presents a thorough discussion of this period, and notes that early Spanish policies required friars to learn local dialects but, at the same time, concluded that vernaculars were not suited for instruction. We find two sets of laws, one requiring the friars to learn the dialects in order to instruct the Filipinos in Christian doctrine, and the other requiring the friars to teach Spanish for the propagation of the Faith (Frei 1959). Spanish policy created a paradoxical situation where it made Spanish an official national language and yet where it was responsible, by missionary policy, for the development of vernacular-Spanish grammars. Colonial policy made Spanish instruction for the natives compulsory after 1588. This policy culminated in the Royal Decree of 1863, which set rules for the establishment of a system of primary instruction that required practical instruction in Spanish. However, the law was never effectively enforced, and local languages continued to be used in the schools (Frei 1959:15). "In theory all children were expected to attend school, but the lower classes displayed considerable reluctance. . . . Thus only a small proportion of the inhabitants made use of the education system established by the Spaniards. . . . The gap between the native upper and lower classes was thereby exacerbated." (Asuncion-Landé 1971:681.) She also notes that while the census of 1960 placed the proportion of Spanish speakers at only 2 percent, the influence that Spanish-speaking Filipinos continued to wield was out of proportion to their numbers.

The gap between upper and lower classes continued when Spanish was replaced by English in the period of American colonialism. American policy—based on the assumptions that although there were numerous vernaculars, none could supplant any other as a common medium of communication, and that regional jealousies and dissensions were to be avoided—chose English as the basic language of instruction and medium of communication. However, as with the case of Spanish, Asuncion-Landé (1971:683) notes that even today

> . . . while English has become a convenient language . . . for the middle and upper classes, it has proved less useful to the lower class. The law stipulating compulsory elementary education could never be strictly enforced. According to the data supplied by the Institute of National Language, 55% of the pupils starting at grade one left school by grade four . . . Though often learning Tagalog through exposure to the entertainment media if they are non-Tagalogs, those who left school before the third grade never acquired enough proficiency in English. Since such . . . serves as a passport to higher positions . . . the educational system, by placing great stress upon English, has underscored the sharp line between the advantaged and the disadvantaged.

By being a language of the Manila area, Tagalog had prominence as a vernacular early in the Spanish period. By the end of the period, with such literate leaders as José Rizal and Emilio Aguinaldo, it became the language of the Philippine Revolution. During the early years of the American adminstration, it was proposed as the national language, but this proposal was rejected by the Philippine Commission, which was the American colonial governing body. Following the establishment of the Philippine Commonwealth in 1935, several policy steps led to the establishment of Tagalog as a core for a national language. First, Article XIII, Section 3, of the Constitution of the Philippines (1936) provided for "development and adoption of a common national language based on one of the existing native languages of the Philippines." The Institute of National Language, created by law in November 1936, with its senior staff selected from speakers of seven leading Philippine vernaculars, was given responsibility for the selection of this language. On December 30, 1936, President Quezon issued Executive Order 134, which proclaimed that Tagalog would be the basis of a national language, and, in April 1940, official authorization was given to the Institute of National Language to publish a Tagalog/English dictionary and a grammar of the (Tagalog-based) Filipino National Language.

However, it was not until the period of Japanese occupation that impetus was given to the recognition of Tagalog, especially by non-Tagalog speakers. The use of English was banned by the Japanese, and the reference to the Filipino National Language was replaced by Tagalog. In an effort to promote the teaching of Japanese, textbooks were prepared in Tagalog, and newspapers featured bilingual Tagalog/Japanese columns. Asuncion-Landé notes that, rather than developing from combined features of other indigenous languages on a Tagalog base, as Philippine officials had planned, the National Language Institute allowed ordinary Tagalog to develop with no prescribed rules. "For the first time in its controversial history as the 'basis' of the national language, the non-Tagalog leaders accepted it unreservedly . . . because they feared the consequence of continuing to use English. But there was also another strong motivation for them to learn it—the conviction that they could unite against a common enemy—the Japanese Occupation Forces" (Asuncion-Landé 1971:685).

The name Tagalog was again changed to Filipino National Language when Philippine independence was proclaimed on July 4, 1946. Along with English, it was designated an official national language. However, under this cumbersome name still lay the real language, Tagalog, which engendered resentment and opposition from non-Tagalogs such that it was renamed Pilipino in 1955. Opposition still exists today, even though national policy has firmly established it as a national language.

Because of a decline in the quality of education after independence, a directive was issued in 1957 that, in non-Tagalog areas, the native language of the area should be the medium of instruction in grades 1 and 2, with English and Tagalog taught as separate subjects. In Tagalog areas, Tagalog should be the medium of instruction in grades 1 and 2, with English taught as a separate subject. Beginning in grade 3, English became the medium of instruction, and Tagalog continued as a separate subject. This policy continued through the 1960s and into the 1970s until, in 1974, a new bilingual education policy was enacted that is still in force today. It is the source of great controversy and is experiencing difficulties in implementation. This policy requires that, beginning in grade 1, Pilipino is to be used as the medium of instruction for social studies, music, art, physical education, and vocational education, and English is to be the medium of instruction for mathematics and science. Depending on the area, either a vernacular or Pilipino is to be used as an auxiliary medium of instruction (Gonzales 1979). Certainly a situation of diglossia, though by no means a stable one, exists in the Philippines today between Pilipino and English.

Resistance to this policy takes many forms. One is clearly regional opposition and fear over possible loss of an international language. Another is over the practical problems of the lack of teachers competent in the subject areas in either Pilipino or English, lack of appropriate texts, and, in the case of Pilipino, lack of appropriate vocabulary (see works by Pineda 1978; Otanes 1978; Enriquez 1978; and Casambre 1978). Several recent studies examine attitudes toward Pilipino. Rachel G. Silliman (1976: 270), in commenting on her study of Bisayan attitudes, notes:

> A majority . . . are of the opinion that a moratorium on the teaching
> of Pilipino (viz., Tagalog) and a reevaluation of the present policy
> are necessary because it has sown discord and encouraged divisiveness.
> They favor the development of a native national language but they
> believe that this language should assimilate lexical entries from other
> Philippine languages, not Tagalog that has simply been relabeled.

This attitude also is expressed in Pineda's summary of the status of the National Language Institute's progress on a Pilipino dictionary that incorporates vocabulary not only from numerous Filipino vernaculars but also from English, Spanish, Japanese, Chinese, and Arabic (Pineda 1978:13). Silliman also notes:

> In spite of strong feelings against Tagalog . . . those interviewed do not belong to an organized group or groups banded expressly to counteract Pilipino. . . . If the subjects resist Pilipino, it comes in the form of apathy toward the language. . . . In many of the respondents, there is a degree of ambivalence. While a national language which is native is desired for symbolic purposes . . . there is also a reluctance to give up English since they are convinced that English is a more useful and practical language that should be learned if the Philippines is to develop economically and to modernize. (1976:270.)

Foley (1976:24) notes in his field study of a Tagalog area that even there, although Pilipino is slowly gaining acceptance, adherence to the present policy in education experiences considerable local variation and, as a language of high prestige and economic advancement, English is strongly preferred by parents and teachers. Bonifacio P. Sibayan perhaps best summarizes the present problems of policy and bilingualism in his study of language use and attitudes:

> The Filipino is confronted with the problem of reconciling the demands made on him by his personal goals, ethnic loyalty, modernization, and nationalism. When the Filipino today says publicly that he prefers to have his child educated in English, he is likely to be misunderstood by staunch nationalists, when all that the average Filipino really wants is to be able to share in the "good life" that is accessible, at least at present through English. And when he says that his next preference for educating his child is his native language, he is yielding to the tug that his ethnicity makes on him. His ethnic loyalty has its origins in a past that includes blood ties, geographic proximity, common customs, and beliefs. . . . If he places Pilipino as his third choice, it is not because he dislikes Pilipino or that he is not patriotic; it is just that his national awareness and identity with the larger society through Pilipino have not yet been sufficiently developed. (1975:129.)

CONCLUSIONS

In comparing the language issues and policies of Spain and the Philippines, some parallels in regionalism are obvious, with four regional groups in Spain and eight dominant groups in the Philippines. However, the parallels cannot be drawn too far, since the situations are somewhat inverse. The Philippines is a new nation in which political unity was formerly imposed from without. Its colonial overlords, through historical accident and bureaucratic convenience or inertia, maintained its geopolitical unity in the face of cultural heterogeneity. It is searching desperately for unifying mechanisms in an attempt to weld its parts into a national whole. A common medium of communication is recognized as an essential step in achieving this goal.

Spain, on the other hand, is one of Europe's older nations, geographically unified for five hundred years. In fact, this unity can be traced back to its status as a western province of the Roman Empire, the source of three of its four languages. Spain exhibits a cultural homogeneity throughout the country. Study after study demonstrate that the values, ideals, and general behavior among the various Spanish regions crosscut regional boundaries. Perhaps the Spanish feel so secure in their national status, each region so interdependent upon the other, that they insist upon the luxury of ethnic integrity, with language diversity symbolic of their sentiments. Nevertheless, there are many within the country who feel that this unity is now threatened by the rise of regional autonomies.

In both nations the dominant language is the one that holds the center of the geographic stage. Tagalog is the language of Manila and environs; Castilian is found in Madrid, while Catalan, Galician, and Basque are peripheral languages. Besides the broad advantages of communication and diffusion that their geographical positions afford them, all capital cities are power centers. The pull of the city is political, but it also spills over into every other facet of life. The educational facilities are centered in Madrid and in Manila, and the effect is to create an intellectual elite.

The central location, the political power, the economic superiority, and the excitement thus generated dictate that the principal centers of media and communication will be there. These become the means of communication for the rest of the nation. The movie industry is also an important consideration. Production of films in Castilian opens up huge markets throughout the world. Movies in Basque or Catalan would have few viewers. While films in Portuguese also would have a large market, the Galician specifically is a lower-class rural inhabitant, hardly addicted to movies. Although films in Tagalog might not have as large an audience as those in Spanish, they are an important entree to the language for non-Tagalog Filipinos. The continued existence of English as an important second language also is bolstered by media considerations in the Philippines.

Factors of diglossia are important in both countries. In Spain, the Catalans and Basques wish to enforce bilingualism on all the inhabitants of their regions, a move opposed by Castilian immigrants to their heavily industrialized urban centers. The Castilians look upon the regional languages as closed systems, the knowledge of which has little real value since the languages themselves are so parochial, on the one hand, while, on the other, all regional speakers are bilingual. Few regional zealots deny the value of retaining Castilian as the national medium of communication.

In the Philippines, the main issues revolve around the dual status of Pilipino and English, but the other principal vernaculars, some of which have their own publication and film industries, will continue to play important roles in the language policies of the nation. While it would be safe to assume that English will probably always be an important language, the unstable political situation in the Muslim regions, the other factors of regionalism, the problems of developing an acceptable phonological, grammatical, and lexical form for Pilipino, and the problems of implementing it as a language of government, business, and education—all make it difficult to predict the long-range future of Pilipino as a national language of the Philippines. In both nations, the issues, as in all pluralistic societies, will always revolve around an interplay between ethnic, national, and international identity.

NOTES

1. The term *diglossia* derives from Ferguson (1959), who coined the term to describe situations where a high or classical standard (such as Koranic Arabic) coexists with a divergent vernacular, being used by bilinguals for different communication domains. However, our use more closely follows Fishman (1967), who has defined the term to include relatively stable and complementary relationships between two or more unrelated

languages in a single society or between two or more code varieties of a single language (see also Gaarder 1977). While the language situations in Spain and the Philippines are not necessarily stable, their national language policies do establish conditions of diglossia.

2. The official term for the Basque language is Euskara. We favor the use of a language term preferred by its speakers; however, since the term is so little known in the United States, we have used Basque. Furthermore, except for most recent decrees, the term used in the *Boletín Oficial del Estado* has been *Vasca*, which translates directly to Basque.

3. Most citations in the discussion of Spain are taken from the *Boletín Oficial del Estado* and translated into English by us. Published weekly, the *Boletín* contains all orders and decrees enacted since the preceding issue. All laws in Spain become effective twenty-four hours after their publication unless otherwise stipulated in the law. When any decree or order is annulled, the law automatically reverts to the previous regulation unless specifically stated otherwise.

Part Two

Implications for Education

Ten Languages or Two? Southern Philippine Multilingualism and Inadequacies in the Philippines' Policy on Bilingual Education

ROBERT A. RANDALL

When one thinks about the policy implications of bilingualism, what comes immediately to mind may well be American policy debates concerning the provision of Spanish-language services to Hispanics or the Canadian policy debates concerning the provision of French services to the Quebecois. For the Philippines, however, the "bilingualism" debate is not about the provision of minority-language services to national minorities but about whether it is desirable and feasible to counter American colonial influence by making education, media, and government services bilingual in English and in Tagalog-based Pilipino. The attempt is to lessen the grip English has on the nation by instituting a dual-language policy. At the same time, however, the bilingualism policy achieves an effect quite opposite to similarly named policies in North America, for Philippine bilingualism policies deliberately restrict access to education, information, and government among those who, for whatever reason, do not know English and Pilipino.

Later I will summarize the history and present status of bilingualism policy and try to explain the thinking of advocates, but here it may be enough to point out some important differences between the North American and Philippine language situations. With nearly fifty million people, the Philippines is the world's seventeenth most populous nation. And as a nation with between forty and eighty mutually unintelligible languages, it experiences interethnic communication difficulties perhaps similar to those in Nigeria, India, Papua New Guinea, and other areas of high linguistic density but several orders of magnitude greater than in North America.

The vast majority of Filipinos speak languages linguistically close to the auxiliary language of Pilipino, and therefore learn it fairly easily. According to recently published research (Frake 1971; Pallesen 1978), however, languages in the south, especially in and around Zamboanga and in the Sulu island chain stretching southwest to Borneo (Philippines Region IX), are rather remotely related to Pilipino. Thus, in Region IX especially, Pilipino has made little progress as an auxiliary language, and the feasibility and desirability of its use in education, government, and media urgently need reconsideration.

THE ZAMBOANGA SPEECH COMMUNITY

Perhaps the easiest way to see why the bilingualism policy needs reconsideration is to examine the linguistic situation in the Zamboanga City area. Here I will briefly describe the history of each language in the area, then indicate its present status in the city, and then discuss the importance the language has for a reference ethnic group—in this case the rural Northern Sinama-speaking Samal fishermen I know best.

The languages that have been in the area the longest are Subanun and the Samalan languages of Yakan and Sinama. Both Subanun and Samal could be indigenous to the area (Frake 1957; Pallesen 1978:166). At present, Subanun is spoken primarily by farmers, plantation workers, and lumber company employees in the interior of the Zamboanga Peninsula, but there are speakers also living in coastal areas as well as a growing number of educated Subanun holding jobs in Zamboanga City. In the city itself, Sinama speakers do not seem to interact much with Subanun.

The Samalan languages are found not only in Region IX but in eastern Malaysia, in eastern Indonesia as far south as Timor and as far north as Kalimantan, in other parts of Mindanao, and in the central Philippines (Pallesen 1978:2).[1] In Zamboanga, there are Yakan and three important dialects of Sinama: Balangingi or Northern, Sibugay Bay, and Central.

Except where intermarried with Sinama, the Yakan have until recently farmed and done business almost exclusively on the island of Basilan just across the strait from Zamboanga. Now, with the continuing military conflict on Basilan, the Yakan have resettled in many places throughout the area. Since Zamboanga-area Sinama shows about 65 percent vocabulary overlap with Yakan (Pallesen 1978:154), what communication difficulties arise between Yakan and Sinama speakers are relatively minor.

The dialects of Sinama are, moreover, subdivided into numerous subdialects that, although linguistically insignificant, have considerable importance in social stratification, political and marital alliances, and in making stereotypic inference. Roughly, the poorest Samal are seminomadic boat people who sell or exchange fish for supplies. The vast majority of Samal are strand dwellers who market fish and coconut and buy goods and services in Zamboanga City. The wealthiest engage in small or even large businesses ranging from cigarette peddling to public transport to long-distance merchandising.

With respect to this merchandising, Samalan males are little different from their ancestors. It seems clear that they have been long-distance traders, slavers, and pirates for at least seven centuries (Fox 1978; Pallesen 1978:341–49). Also, because Samal engage in fishing and marine-product merchandising, they are less tied to the land than are most peoples and so tend to move relatively easily and frequently. This has produced a large number of geographically disperse Samalan languages with extensive convergent borrowing from other languages in lexicon and syntax.[2] And this, in turn, makes it unusually difficult to understand the relation of Sinama and Yakan to the other Philippine languages.

In any case, sometime in the twelfth century, some traveling Samal traders evidently married women speaking a language related to Butuanun, an Eastern Mindanao language related to Cebuano Bisayan and ultimately to Central Philippines languages such as Tagalog (Pallesen 1978:24–28). The Samal traders took these women back to Jolo Island southwest of Zamboanga, and in time their descendants came to speak Tausug. Today, Tausug is spoken not only in Jolo but in most of the Muslim areas in and around Zamboanga. Many Tausug are wealthy and therefore politically, religiously, and socially influential. They also continue to marry Samal and Yakan, and so their language is of considerable importance to Samal.

From the viewpoint of Sinama speakers, competence in Tausug often comes from exposure to relatives or to neighbors, from political or economic allies and benefactors, from media—particularly the popular Tausug opera records—and from the Tausug-dominated "high" Muslim religious observances broadcast on TV and radio. In my experience, most Samal men and many women speak and understand some Tausug, but few are really competent. The converse is also true of Tausug knowledge of Sinama, and so communication is easy for some and difficult for others.

Islamic observances occur not only in Sinama, Yakan, and Tausug, but also, of course, in Arabic. Arabic has been in the area for six centuries or more, and is constitutionally recognized as a national language. No one speaks it as a first language, but an increasing number of people who have resided in the Arabic-speaking world are using it in religious contexts and a considerable minority study enough Arabic to recite the Koran (Molony 1969:105). Since educated Muslims are being hired for work in Kuwait, and since Arabic retains prestige in the adjacent Muslim nations of Indonesia and Malaysia, it seems likely that knowledge of Arabic will continue to be a goal of many Zamboanga area people.

Various Chinese languages constitute another class of languages having considerable antiquity in Zamboanga. Hokkien, Cantonese, and others are spoken not only by recent Chinese immigrants but by descendants of those who settled in centuries past. Chinese linguistic contact is at least seven hundred years old (Pallesen 1978:9), and could be three times older. In Zamboanga today, much business is owned by the Chinese, and there are many other Chinese-owned or -influenced institutions as well. Since Chinese often marry speakers of indigenous Philippine languages, the native-born are often fluent multilinguals. I know, for example, a Cantonese-Sinama man who is married to a Hokkien-Bisayan. Samal commonly shop at Chinese stores, borrow money at Chinese pawnshops, sell their coconut to Chinese traders, and frequently work for Chinese. In all cases, Philippine languages are used to communicate.

Spanish was introduced into the area with colonization in the early 1700s. Today, contrary to a prevalent American misconception, it is not widely spoken in the Philippines. What is spoken in a few areas throughout the nation is a Spanish-Philippine creole known as Chabacano. Frake (1971), who has studied the language, says it derives from the Hilagaynon Bisayan, Tagalog, and Spanish used in eighteenth-century fort settlements. Today, there are some 100,000 speakers of a Zamboangueño dialect, having an 80–90 percent Spanish lexicon but largely Philippine syntax.

Zamboangueño is currently the dominant language in Zamboanga City, parts of Basilan, and many rural farming villages. Although some Chabacanos learn Spanish in school and there continue to be Spanish missionaries in the areas, it is of minor importance. By contrast, most Samal who live near the city know enough Zamboangueño to give directions to a driver, to explain themselves to the police, to buy stamps or lumber, to court, and to talk with a schoolmate, boss, or friend.

English also entered with colonization and, along with the Tagalog-based Pilipino, is today one of the two constitutionally recognized languages used in education. In Zamboanga, it sometimes operates as an auxiliary language, and is common in films, print media, and in a wide variety of government printing activities. At the present time, very few Sinama speakers can converse in English, but most children are learning some in the schools, and nearly all adults regard English as an economically and politically valuable skill.

In recent years as well, increasing numbers of people from outside the region have been emigrating into or working in the area. Of these, Bisayans from the central Philippines are probably the most numerous and important. In the rural Samal experience, it would be useful to speak Bisayan in order to converse with physicians, teachers, military officers, fishing boat captains, and others in high status occupations.

There also, of course, have been visitors from other Philippine language areas and from outside the country. In this latter category, the Japanese have been increasing a presence that predates their World War II occupation. Also, as a result of Manila policies, non-English-speaking Europeans are touring Zamboanga in increasing numbers. The impact of these languages, however, is so far minor. Although those Samal who work for the Japanese pearl farm or who act as guides and peddlers in the tourist trade have great difficulty communicating with those that hire them, most Samal simply avoid interaction with foreigners.

Two other languages not really spoken in the area are, nevertheless, important. Malay is not spoken in the Philippines, but several factors are increasing its relative importance to Zamboanga Muslims. In particular, the oil and lumber boom in Malaysian Borneo together with the military stalemate in the southern Philippines have made residence in east Malaysia attractive to an estimated 100,000. I have talked to many Samal who have lived a year or so in Borneo and then returned briefly to visit their families. Obviously, many Samal are learning some Malay.

Last, but by no means least, every schoolchild is being taught Pilipino. Although few people in Zamboanga speak it as a first language, at least some can use it as an auxiliary language when necessary. Sinama speakers also hear Pilipino in movies and occasionally read it in comics and magazines. In recent years, some villagers have been exposed to it by interacting with occupying soldiers, and a few have used it when visiting Manila, but most Sinama speakers seem to regard it as just one of many languages.

To sum up then, there are at least ten languages spoken either as a first language or as an auxiliary language by significant numbers of people in Zamboanga: Arabic, Bisayan, "Chinese," English, Pilipino, Sinama, Subanun, Tausug, Yakan, and Zamboangueño. Arabic, Chinese, and English are completely unrelated to Philippine languages and to each other, and Zamboangueño is only remotely related to English and the Philippine languages. Of the remainder, Tausug and Bisayan are closely related and so are Yakan and the Sinama languages, but both Pilipino and Subanun are not very closely related to any Zamboanga language. Table 1 uses data provided by Pallesen (1978:151), Dyen (1965), and Frake (1971) to summarize lexical similarities. Since two language varieties must have 70–80 percent cognate vocabulary with similar meaning to be mutually intelligible (cf. Dyen 1965:16), it should be obvious how dissimilar the Zamboanga languages are. In particular, the Samalan languages are somewhat more closely related to Malay than to Bisayan and, despite Tausug's long contact with Sinama, it shares 50 percent more

Table 1. Percentages of Shared Lexicon for Related Zamboanga City Languages (from Pallesen 1978:151–154; Frake 1971; Dyen 1965)

LANGUAGE	North Sinama	Central Sinama	Sibugay Bay Sinama	Yakan	Malay	Subanun	Tausug (193-word list)	Tausug (372-word list)	Bisayan (Cebuano)	Pilipino (Tagalog)
SAMALAN:										
SINAMA:										
Northern Sinama (Balangingi)										
Central Sinama	77									
Sibugay Bay Sinama	66	63								
Yakan	62	62	59							
Malay	?	27	?	25						
MESO-PHILIPPINES:										
Subanun	?	29	29	29	?					
CENTRAL PHILIPPINES										
NORTHEASTERN MINDANAO:										
Tausug(193-word list)	36	37	24	33	?	?				
Tausug (372-word list)	45	45	25	36	?	?				
Bisayan (Cebuano)	25	25	25	23	<23	45	68	?		
Pilipino (Tagalog)	<23	<23	<23	<23	<23	45	?	?	54	
Zamboangueño	<5	<5	<5	<5	<5	<5	?	?	10–20	10–20

vocabulary with Bisayan than it does with Sinama. In general, the main Zamboanga languages do not share much vocabulary either with each other or with the main languages of the north.

INTERETHNIC COMMUNICATION PROBLEMS IN ZAMBOANGA

There is no need to dwell on the obvious. With such linguistic diversity in contact, there are bound to be major communication problems. Here I want to cite a few examples of what such facts can mean in people's daily lives.

One Sinama-speaking village prefers having Bisayan teachers in the primary school, even though they do not speak Sinama and therefore cannot communicate effectively with entering primary students. When asked, a village official said that, given the tense military situation, it was advisable to have a Bisayan around who would be trusted by the military and who could effectively communicate with officers should an "operation" be launched.

A Pampamgueño who is fluent in Chabacano and several other languages was nevertheless amazed to learn what was being gossiped everywhere in the Sinama-speaking community: that a protracted war was being waged some twenty miles away between the military and the Moro National Liberation Front.

The Hokkien-Bisayan woman I mentioned earlier confided that she understands neither her Sinama-speaking mother-in-law nor her Hokkien grandmother.

A Bisayan lieutenant colonel told me he used to think he understood the Tausug language until he studied an anthropology book in defense college and learned differently.

A Samal politician misunderstood this same lieutenant colonel's English, particularly an unwillingness by the officer to accept personal rather than organizational responsibility for improved relations between Samal and the military.

Samal men consistently pay 5 percent per month interest at pawnshops even though their pawn ticket clearly says in English that 2.5 percent is the maximum allowed. Quite obviously, the ability to switch linguistic codes is often of considerable importance to

Zamboanga people. From the Sinama viewpoint, "Chinese" and Subanun languages can be ignored, but the remaining languages cannot be.

THE PHILIPPINE POLICY ON BILINGUAL EDUCATION

One would hope, of course, that language education policies could somehow be designed to provide Zamboanga people with the language skills needed to live in Zamboanga.[3] In this respect it is instructive to look at policies Manila is attempting to implement in the area. In general, they were formulated as national policies with apparently little informed knowledge about whether they were feasible or desirable in the Zamboanga area. Given the recent date of relevant research, this is hardly surprising.

Instead, it seems to have been assumed from the start that Philippine citizens would need to know just one vernacular language in addition to English and Pilipino. Essentially, the current language policy is a reflection of the 1973 Constitution, the National Board of Education's declared policy on English/Pilipino bilingualism, and the Department of Education and Culture's implementation guidelines (Department Order No. 9, s.1973; No. 25, s.1974). The goal is to "develop a bilingual nation competent in the use of both English and Pilipino . . . [and] Arabic . . . where it is necessary." And this is to be done by using particular languages to teach particular subject areas: English in science and mathematics; Pilipino in social studies and social science, character education, work education, health education, and physical education. In grades 1 and 2 only, "the vernacular used in the locality or place where the school is located shall be the auxiliary medium of instruction . . . when necessary to facilitate understanding. . . ." According to plan, the policy should be working nationwide from Grade 1 through the fourth year of high school by 1984, but implementation is lagging in Regions I (Kalinga-Apay), VII (central Visayas), and IX (Zamboanga and the southwest) (A. Gonzales 1979).

The rationale behind the plan seems straightforward enough. President Quezon selected Tagalog in the 1930s as the basis for Pilipino. Pilipino education is necessary to counter the overwhelming "miseducation" caused by Anglicization and American colonial domination (E. Gonzales 1975:1). At the same time, it is not feasible and there is no consensus to abandon English, and so English will continue to be taught. Since the simultaneous use of two languages can easily lead to language creolization (E. Gonzales 1975) and is in fact leading to "adulterated language which is neither English nor Pilipino" (See Manuel 1978), it is judged necessary to keep instruction in both languages rigorously separated by subject matter. Finally, since the prepubescent learn languages with comparative ease, instruction should ". . . introduce the child early in life to the languages that he would need in later years in Philippine society—English and Pilipino in addition to the vernacular" (E. Gonzales 1975:3–4). Hence, Pilipino and English media instruction should ideally be the only languages used from Grade 1 on.

INADEQUACIES IN THE BILINGUAL INSTRUCTION POLICY IN ZAMBOANGA

What should be obvious from my discussion is that Pilipino and English are not the languages the vast majority of Zamboanga people will "need" most in later years. From a strictly practical viewpoint, nearly everyone in the area would benefit far more by education in any of several languages actually used in the area. Fluency in Zamboangueño, Sinama, Tausug, or Subanun could easily double the number of people one could obtain services from, do business with, and have peaceful relations with. By contrast, both English and Pilipino are important to the vast majority without higher education, not because "one needs them in later years," but mainly because there are few if any printed materials in vernacular languages. If there were such materials, however, it seems highly likely that the Samal and others would learn a great deal more about health, Philippine history, science, technology, their fellow southerners, and even northerners than they now do.

SOME REFLECTIONS ON THE BILINGUALISM POLICY

What then should be done? As an outsider in a nation where Americans are rightly accused of meddling too much, I know that

Major Ethnic Linguistic Groups in the Philippines.

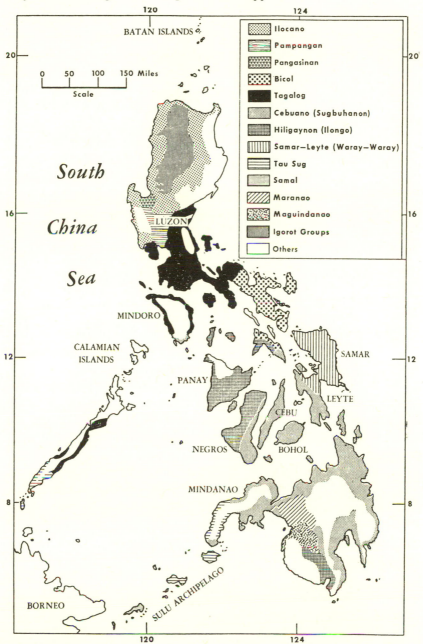

Legend:
- Ilocano
- Pampangan
- Pangasinan
- Bicol
- Tagalog
- Cebuano (Sugbuhanon)
- Hiligaynon (Ilongo)
- Samar—Leyte (Waray—Waray)
- Tau Sug
- Samal
- Maranao
- Maguindanao
- Igorot Groups
- Others

Source: Federic H. Chaffee, George E. Aurell, Helen A. Barth, Elinor C. Betters, Ann S. Cort, John H. Dombrowski, Vincent J. Fasano and John O. Weaver, 1969. *Area Handbook for the Philippines* (Washington, D.C.: U.S. Government Printing Office).

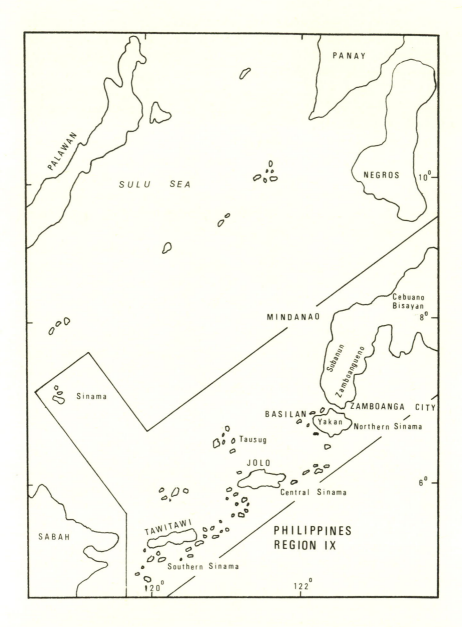

PANAY

PALAWAN

SULU SEA

NEGROS 10°

Cebuano
Bisayan
MINDANAO 8°

Subanun

Zamboangueno

ZAMBOANGA CITY

BASILAN Yakan Northern Sinama

Sinama

Tausug

JOLO

Central Sinama 6°

TAWITAWI

SABAH

PHILIPPINES
REGION IX

Southern Sinama

120° 122°

it is not my role to make recommendations. But as an anthropological linguist who has been privileged to work, live, and study in the Philippines, I feel it appropriate to share some of my observations. First, it seems obvious that a much more systematic study of the linguistic needs of Zamboanga should be made. If it is true, as seems probable, that Pilipino and English are not being used as much as many other languages in the area, it may well be that the often cited lack of motivation to learn Pilipino (E. Gonzales 1975:6) is not so much due to resistance and the political situation (A. Gonzales 1979) as it is to the objective language situation itself. Can the Samal be expected to learn Pilipino, English, Arabic, Zamboangueño, Tausug, and Sinama when not one of these languages shares 40 percent vocabulary with any other?

In my view, some serious reconsideration of the bilingual instruction policy is necessary in areas where there are several auxiliary and vernacular languages radically different from Pilipino. Rather than opting to push Pilipino where it may simply not be feasible, it may make more sense to make more use of selected vernaculars. In doing so, the Philippines might avoid some of the problems India has experienced pushing Hindi in Dravidian areas. At the same time, it could learn from Nigeria's experience with instruction both in English and in four indigenous auxiliary languages.

NOTES

1. Although I have spent more than a decade studying Sinama (through the auspices of the National Science Foundation and a University of Houston Research Initiation Grant), most of my understanding of the status of Samalan languages comes from Pallesen's outstanding monograph (1978).

2. For example, Sinama has significant Malay and Tausug borrowings (Pallesen 1978), and a Samalan language in the Moluccas is without syntactic features found in the Zamboanga area (Charles Frake, personal communication).

3. Much of my understanding of bilingualism policy is due to the information generously provided by Dr. Pablo E. Natividad of the Curriculum Development Division of the Bureau of Elementary Education in the Ministry of Education and Culture. What I say here regarding Zamboanga is, however, unrelated to the considerable help he gave me in understanding the government's present policy.

Alphabets and National Policy:
The Case of Guaraní

Louisa R. Stark

Paraguay is one of the few truly bilingual countries in the world. Statistics vividly show that only 8 percent of the population are monolingual in Spanish, whereas 92 percent are capable of speaking Guaraní. This number can be broken down into 52 percent who are bilingual in Guaraní and Spanish and 40 percent who are monolingual in Guaraní. The latter are primarily rural peasants, whereas the former are scattered throughout the country. This situation appears to have undergone minimal change since the 1950s (Academy for Educational Development 1977:A-7).

Paraguay has declared Spanish to be its Official Language, whereas Guaraní is the country's national language. In so doing, Paraguay has stressed its role as a bilingual nation in which speaking Guaraní and Spanish is to be esteemed. Guaraní alone is not thought to have any inherent value in its own right. Thus a person who speaks only Guaraní is *Guarango* (ill-bred, bore), and *menos inteligente* (less intelligent) or *menos desarrollado* (less developed) than a person who is bilingual or even monolingual in Spanish. Monolingual speakers often share this deprecatory attitude and call themselves *tavɨ* (stupid) because they cannot speak Spanish (Rubin 1968:46). One also is described, and will describe oneself, as uneducated and uncultivated if one speaks only Guaraní. This stems from the fact that it is in school that the monolingual Guaraní speaker generally has his or her first exposure to Spanish, and it is here that the language is learned. Thus the assumption is made that the person who does not speak Spanish is the person who has not had much formal education. "Amount of schooling is the single most important factor in determining Spanish proficiency" (Rubin 1968:84).

However, there are certain factors that hinder the learning of Spanish, or of any other subject, by the 90 percent of rural children who enter the school system speaking only Guaraní (Academy for Educational Development 1977:A-11). The monolingual child entering the first grade is confronted not only with the foreign culture of the school but also with a completely foreign language—Spanish—in which all instruction is carried out. The child finding himself or herself in such a position either drops out of school or is withdrawn by his or her parents, who realize that he or she is not profiting from the experience. The result is that in the first grade in the rural schools alone, approximately 30 percent of all children drop out of school, with another 30 percent having to repeat the first grade (Weil et al. 1973:100). Therefore, for 60 percent of the children attending the first grade in any rural school, their first year of formal education is a disaster.

Thus we have a situation in Paraguay where great numbers of rural school children, most of them monolingual in Guaraní, are either dropping out or not being promoted within the elementary school system. This has resulted in severe sociocultural, as well as economic, discrimination against the uneducated monolingual speaker of Guaraní. And it has provided Paraguay with an illiteracy rate of 25 percent (Secretaría General de la Organización de los Estados Americanos, 1973:7).

Recently the Paraguayan government has recognized the problems of educating its monolingual Guaraní-speaking population and has been attempting to come to grips with those problems. However, as one ministry official privately said, "Our hearts seem to be in the right place, but we simply don't know how to proceed with devising the kind of educational curriculum that the vast number of our rural children seem to need" (anonymous informant).

In order to help remedy this situation, the United States Agency for International Development (USAID) suggested to the Paraguayan Ministry of Education (MOE) the possibility of collaborating on the development of a program in bilingual education, to be implemented in the first three years of primary school in the rural areas of the country, to begin in 1979. The MOE accepted the proposal and put together a team that, in collaboration with foreign advisers contracted by USAID, were in charge of developing the plan. It would be a maintenance-type program. Beginning in the first grade, instruction would be carried out in Guaraní while children concurrently received instruction in oral Spanish. In the second grade, instruction would be continued in oral Spanish while the rest of the curriculum would be taught bilingually in Guaraní and Spanish. Finally, in the third grade, basic classroom instruction would be in Spanish, with supplementary materials in Guaraní.

This kind of program, of course, would entail the preparation of teaching materials in Guaraní. According to the MOE personnel associated with the project, this could be a great problem, since there were currently in Paraguay seven competing alphabets for the writing of the language, each with its devoted partisans. And each presents a variety of different symbols for the representation of Guaraní sounds that do not have equivalents in Spanish.

In some cases, symbols derived from Spanish are used to represent different sounds in Guaraní. For example, in the alphabet developed by Padre Guasch, the symbol x stands for /š/, while in Spanish the same symbol indicates the consonant cluster /ks/. On the other hand, the same sound in both languages has often been represented by different graphemes. Thus in the orthography commonly used by songwriters, Guaraní j and Spanish y indicate the phoneme /ǰ/ with the problem compounded since j usually represents the phoneme /x/ in Spanish. Beyond this, there is the problem that native speakers of Guaraní, perhaps because of the plethora of competing alphabets to which they have been subjected, in one sentence or phrase will write the same Guaraní sounds with a variety of symbols gathered from a variety of alphabets. In other words, there is little consistency in the writing of Guaraní.

Since Paraguay has declared itself officially to be a bilingual nation, it seems imperative that, in developing teaching materials for use in the country's classrooms, an alphabet should be used in Guaraní that does not conflict with that used in the writing of Spanish. The MOE team decided to design such an alphabet, which would be used exclusively for teaching primary-school children to read. It would be analogous to the traditional way of teaching English-speaking children to read using phonics, with the idea that in both cases the child could at a later stage more easily master the more traditional ways of writing the language. Developing a transitional

alphabet would alleviate having to choose one of the already existing alphabets, which, although such a choice would satisfy the
proponents of that particular orthography, would surely displease
supporters of the other six. It was also believed that, by presenting
the MOE alphabet as a transition orthography, supporters of the
other seven would feel assured that their own would be better learned,
at least eventually, by the children coming out of the bilingual
program.

With these goals in mind, an alphabet was designed by the MOE
Bilingual Education team, using the following symbols for phonemes in Guaraní not found in Spanish:

SOUND   GRAPHEME

/k/ Although the c was adopted because of its conformity
with the Spanish alphabet, Spanish qu has been replaced   k/-i,e,ï/
by k because it was felt that it would be easier to teach   c/-u,o,a/
first-graders to use one symbol (k) before /i,e,ï/ instead
of two (qu), as in traditional Spanish orthography.

/h/ This sound is currently represented as an h or jh in Guar-   x
aní orthographies. However, since Spanish /x/ and Guar-
aní are close phonetically (a voiceless velar fricative versus
a voiceless glottal fricative), it was decided that perhaps
the symbol j could be used to represent Guaraní /h/. This
would circumvent problems that would arise using h,
which does not indicate a sound in Spanish, and h indicating a glottal fricative in Guaraní. The use of jh was
also considered, but was thought to be more difficult to
teach because of its compound nature and because it could
be confused with j and h of Spanish, each of which has
a distinct phonetic equivalent.

/š/ Traditionally there have been three ways of representing   sh
the voiceless alveopalatal sibilant in Guaraní: x, ch, and
sh, with x and ch most commonly used. However, since
x and ch represent different sounds (/ks/, /č/) in Spanish,
it was decided that sh would be more acceptable and less
confusing to use in the writing of school texts.

/ǰ/ Both Spanish and Guaraní have a voiced alveopalatal af-   y
fricated stop /ǰ/, which in Paraguayan Spanish orthography is written using the symbol y. In Guaraní, both j and
y have been used to represent this sound. For the teaching of Guaraní in the schools, it was felt that y would be
a better choice since it symbolizes a similar sound in
Spanish.

/ɨ/ This sound fluctuates between a high central unrounded   ɨ
vocoid and a mid central unrounded vocoid. Tradition-
ally it has been represented as y. However, because of
the confusion that results from using y to represent /ɨ/ in
Guaraní and /ǰ/ in Spanish, it was decided to adopt the
crossed i (ɨ) to indicate the Guaraní vowel.

/Ṽ/ Traditionally nasalized vowels have been indicated by   ṽ
using a tilde or accent circumflex. Since the tilde is more
commonly used to indicate nasalization and is also used
in Portuguese, it was selected for the writing of Guaraní.

After designing a potential alphabet for use in teaching primary
school children to read Guaraní, the MOE Bilingual Education team
decided to test this orthography on a small group of students in
order to have an indication of its merits and problems and to compare the results with the two most popular traditional alphabets: that
of the Academia Guaraní (AG), and that known as the Popular, the
alphabet used for the transcription of songs and popular poetry. If
it could be proved that primary-school children could more easily
read in the transitional orthography, then partisans of the other two
could not be as upset over the fact that their own alphabet was not
chosen for use in the preparation of educational materials.

The following chart shows the main differences between the three
spelling systems.

PHONEME	AG	POPULAR	TRANSITIONAL ALPHABET DESIGNED BY MOE TEAM
/k/	k	c/k	c/k
/h/	h	jh	j
/š/	ch	ch	sh
/ǰ/	j	y	y
/ɨ/	y	y	ï
/ṽ/	Ṽ	V̂	Ṽ

Basically there are two methods that one can use to test the readability of a practical writing system. The first and most nearly ideal
is to teach alternative systems of writing to two or more different
groups using identical materials but with different orthographies.
After one or two years, the reading abilities of the two groups can
be compared to determine which alphabet has been the most successful (Venezky 1970).

The second method is to teach groups of readers of an official language the graphemes of the first language in one of the alternative spelling systems. Then, using paragraphs of varying semantic complexity, the readers would be tested on the readability of each system, being rated on mispronunciations, substitutions, omissions, repetitions, and comprehension. Because of the urgency to begin the preparation of teaching materials in Guaraní, it was decided to use the second method for testing the effectiveness of the MOE-developed alphabet.

The test was developed and carried out in the following way. (1) The students selected for the test were from the fourth grade, of ages nine through eleven, and were divided equally between boys and girls. It was felt that, by the fourth grade, students should have the reading ability in Spanish to be able to participate in the Guaraní test. A total of seventy-two students participated, of which twenty-four tested in each of the Guaraní orthographies; twelve were girls, and twelve were boys. (2) The test was applied to three rural schools. In each school a fourth-grade teacher was asked to select his/her best-reading students in Spanish who were also bilingual in that language and Guaraní. The investigator, a Paraguayan teacher herself, would then select at random from this group six boys and six girls. (3) Each student was asked to read a passage in Spanish. The passage was from a fourth-grade reader that was not currently in use in the school system. The student was permitted to read the passage first in silence and then aloud, so as to judge his or her reading ability. If the student made more than ten mistakes (mispronunciations, repetitions, or omissions) while reading the Spanish-language passage, he or she was judged ineligible to continue with the reading test in Guaraní. For those who continued, each of the three Guaraní orthographies was then tested on four children, two boys and two girls. (4) The first stage of the reading test consisted of a series of single words, each representing a concept well known to a Guaraní-speaking child. The tester reviewed the words with the student. Where there were symbols that the student did not already command, the investigator taught the child informally the symbol-sound correspondence in the particular Guaraní writing system in which the student would be tested. (5) After this part of the investigation, the student was given a short text in Guaraní and was asked first to read it silently and then read it aloud. The text, written in colloquial Guaraní, or Jopará, involved an everyday situation in the life of a rural child. The student was asked to read the text first silently and then aloud, at which point it was taped. (6) Finally, the student was asked questions relating to the text so as to measure his or her comprehension of what had been read.

Back at the Ministry, the taped oral readings were evaluated for reading proficiency using criteria based on a modification of the Goodman Miscue Inventory (Goodman and Burke 1972; Stark 1977a). Mispronunciations, substitutions, omissions, and repetitions were noted, with repetitions and mispronunciations receiving twice the value of errors of omission and substitution. The total number of mistakes made in reading each grapheme was then divided into the total number of occurrences of the grapheme in the text in order to arrive at the percentage of mistakes made. These were then averaged for the twenty-four readers of each alphabet and the results compared across alphabets between graphemes representing the same sound.

The following were the results:

(1) The voiceless velar stop /k/
   This sound occurred four times in each of the texts; the percentage of errors in reading each grapheme was the following.

	GRAPHEME	PERCENTAGE OF ERRORS
Experimental Alphabet	c (+ a,u,o)	4.9
	k (+ i,i,e)	
AG Alphabet	k	3.3
Popular Alphabet	c (+ a,u,o)	6.5
	k (+ y,i,e)	

Interpretation: Readers had somewhat less difficulty with the reading of k in all environments, as contrasted with c and k in distinctive environments.

(2) The voiceless glottal fricative /h/
   This sound occurred eleven times in each of the texts; the percentage of errors in reading each grapheme was the following.

	GRAPHEME	PERCENTAGE OF ERRORS
Experimental Alphabet	j	14.0
AG Alphabet	h	23.7
Popular Alphabet	jh	22.9

Interpretation: Here there was a statistically significant difference between the ease with which the readers interpreted the grapheme indicating the voiceless glottal fricative in the Experimental alphabet (14.0 percent) and the difficulties encountered in reading the graphemes of the AG and Popular alphabets (23.7 percent and 22.9 percent, respectively). In the AG alphabet, the readers generally interpreted the symbol h as indicating Ø, since this symbol in Spanish is not pronounced. In the Popular alphabet, there was a tendency on the part of the readers to pronounce the combination jh as /ǰ/. The symbol that was read with greatest ease was the j of the Experimental alphabet, because of its equivalence with the symbol used to indicate the voiceless velar fricative in Spanish (example: hijo /ixo/"son").

(3) The voiceless alveopalatal sibilant /š/
This phoneme occurred five times in each of the three texts; the percentage of errors in the reading of each grapheme was the following.

	GRAPHEME	PERCENTAGE OF ERRORS
Experimental Alphabet	sh	12.1
AG Alphabet	ch	17.3
Popular Alphabet	ch	7.8

Interpretation: It is difficult to explain why there was such a discrepancy in the reading of the same grapheme, ch, in the AG and Popular alphabets. The reason for the fair amount of ease in reading the symbol probably comes from phonological interference between Spanish and Guaraní. The average incipient Spanish speaker who is a native speaker of Guaraní pronounces Spanish /č/ as /š/. Thus he or she pronounces the Spanish word *muchacho* /mučačo/ as /mušašo/, *mucho* /mučo/ as /mušo/, et cetera. Since the Guaraní-speaking child tends to pronounce Spanish words written with ch as /š/, he or she will tend to do the same when reading Guaraní words written with ch. However, if one were to use the symbol ch when introducing Guaraní literacy to indicate the phoneme /š/, as well as to use the same symbol to indicate the /č/ of Spanish, one would simply be reinforcing the oral pronunciation of Spanish /č/ as Guaraní /š/, not only strengthening nonstandard patterns of pronunciation in Spanish but also adding to the problems of teaching literacy in that language.

(4) The voiced alveopalatal affricated stop /ǰ/

This phoneme occurred seven times in each of three texts; the percentage of errors in the reading of each grapheme was the following.

	GRAPHEME	PERCENTAGE OF ERRORS
Experimental Alphabet	y	8.7
AG Alphabet	j	38.5
Popular Alphabet	y	24.6

Interpretation: Readers had the greatest amount of trouble interpreting the j of the AG alphabet; the majority of them pronounced it as /x/ because of its equivalence with the grapheme j that is used to indicate the voiceless velar fricative in Spanish (example: hijo /ixo/ son). Readers had less difficulty reading the grapheme y, because it indicates the same sound (/ǰ/) in Paraguayan Spanish. However, there is a fairly large statistical difference between the 8.7 percent errors made in reading the symbol in the Experimental orthography and the 24.6 percent encountered in the Popular orthography. This may be attributed to the fact that the Popular orthography also uses the grapheme y to indicate the high back unrounded vowel /ï/. However, even with the problem of using the same grapheme to represent two sounds in the language, there were fewer mistakes (24.6 percent) reading the y in the Popular orthography than the j (38.5 percent) in the AG alphabet. And when y indicates only one phoneme, the voiceless alveopalatal affricated stop, the percentage of mistakes fell to 8.7 percent.

(5) The high back unrounded vowel /ï/

This phoneme occurred eight times in each of the three texts; the percentage of errors in the reading of each grapheme was as follows.

	GRAPHEME	PERCENTAGE OF ERRORS
Experimental Alphabet	ɨ	20.9
AG Alphabet	y	16.2
Popular Alphabet	y	35.3

Interpretation: As can be seen by the percentages, both the highest and the lowest number of reading mistakes occurred with the grapheme y; in the AG alphabet this totaled 16.2 percent, and in the Popular the total was 35.3 percent. The explanation for the high number of mistakes in the Popular alphabet is that the y was used in that alphabet to indicate both the consonant phoneme /ǰ/ as well as the vowel /ï/. (This also provided a large number of problems for readers of that alphabet in their interpretation of y when it stood for the phoneme /ǰ/; see [4] above.) The lower number of mistakes with y indicating /ï/ occurred in the AG alphabet when the grapheme did not represent a second sound as well.

However, in spite of the slightly lower number of mistakes in the use of y in the AG (16.2 percent) than in the use of ɨ in the Experimental alphabet (20.9 percent), the choice of y to represent /ï/ should probably be avoided. For if y is chosen to represent both /ï/ and /ǰ/, then the total percentage of reading errors in the interpretation of both phonemes rises dramatically.

	/ï/	/ǰ/
Popular Alphabet	y (35.3 percent)	y (24.6 percent)

Moreover, if y is used to represent the vowel /ï/, and a symbol other than y is used to indicate the affricated stop /ǰ/, the reader will have problems interpreting the symbol representing the consonant.

	/ï/	/ǰ/
AG Alphabet	y (16.2 percent)	j (38.5 percent)

If a symbol such as ɨ is used to represent the vowel /ɨ/, and y is used to indicate the affricated stop /ǰ/, as in Paraguayan Spanish, then the reader has few problems in interpreting the consonant (8.7 percent) and only a slightly higher percentage of errors in interpreting the ɨ (20.9 percent) than the vowel symbol y (16.2 percent) representing only one sound in the AG alphabet. Thus the ease in interpreting the consonant when written as y more than outbalances the small span of difference between reading the vowel when written as y as it occurs in the AG alphabet (16.2 percent) and the ɨ in the Experimental alphabet (20.9 percent).

	/ɨ/	/ǰ/
Experimental Alphabet	ɨ (20.9 percent)	y (8.7 percent)

(6) Nasalization of Vowels /Ṽ/

Nasalized vowels occurred five times in each of the texts, and the percentage of errors in reading each grapheme was the following.

	GRAPHEME	PERCENTAGE OF ERRORS
Experimental Alphabet	˜	7.4
AG Alphabet	˜	6.0
Popular Alphabet	ˆ	9.13

Interpretation: Although the readers had somewhat less difficulty with the tilde than with the circumflex, statistically the difference was not that great. The tilde may have been somewhat easier for the readers because of its association with the nasal grapheme ñ in Spanish, whereas the circumflex was an entirely new symbol.

Several principles for the development of orthographies, which up until now have not been tested scientifically, were reinforced by the results of the reading tests. (1) One sound should be represented by one symbol. When a phoneme is represented by more than one letter, it is more difficult to read, as in the case of Guaraní /k/ being represented as both k (before /i,e,ɨ/) and c (before /u,o,a/). It is interesting to note that although the Guaraní-speaking students had mastered the use of qu and c to represent /k/ in Spanish, they still had a hard time reading k and c when they symbolized the same phoneme, /k/, in Guaraní. (2) Two different sounds should be represented by two distinct symbols. When two sounds are represented by one symbol, they are much more difficult to read. This was the case with y when it was used to represent both /ɨ/ and /ǰ/ in the Popular alphabet. (3) Similar sounds in the nation's official and unofficial languages are best represented by the same or similar symbols. In the case of Guaraní /ǰ/ and Spanish /ǰ/, reading was easier when the same symbol was used for both sounds. Even for analogous sounds, when the same letter j was used to represent Guaraní /h/ and Spanish /x/, there was more ease of reading than when totally different symbols were used for the same phonemes. And, finally, it was easier to read nasalized vowels marked with a tilde in Guaraní, rather than with a circumflex, because of the association of the former symbol with the alveopalatal nasal ñ in Spanish.

To conclude, the testing of the experimental orthography not only served to prove its worth vis-à-vis the other two alphabets but, for the first time, generated statistical data that reinforce certain common axioms for the development of practical writing systems.

With the results of the tests, the MOE team had the data needed not only for the development of a transitional alphabet but also to counteract those critics who would prefer one of the country's other writing systems. At least on the surface, this should have been the situation, but such was not the case. When the results of the tests came in, there was a feeling of profound discomfort on the part of the MOE team. Although as a group they had developed the Experimental alphabet, almost every member believed that it would have been better if one of the other two orthographies had "won." Some were personally partial to one alphabet or the other, but in general there was the sudden realization that there would be an enormous amount of criticism of the experimental writing system as well as of the team that had developed it. This would come not only from partisans of the Popular alphabet but, even more seriously, from those who had developed the orthography of the Academia Guaraní, an old and venerated group made up of the country's most distinguished writers and linguists.

Beyond this, there was the realization that having proved that children could read successfully in a transitional alphabet, the myth that conflicting orthographies in Guaraní made it impossible to teach basic literacy in that language would have to be dispelled. A successful orthography would destroy this belief but, in so doing, would run into political opposition on the part of the country's government. For by keeping a large sector of the population monolingual in Guaraní and illiterate in both Spanish and Guaraní, the government can easily control the information that this sector of the population receives. Until now, what had been written in Guaraní was almost totally in the form of music, poetry, and humor, as was true of radio programs in that language. In order to gain news of goings-on in the country, one must both read and understand Spanish; otherwise, one was cut off from national and international events.

A person who participates in a well-developed bilingual education program should, in a short period of time, be able to read and write in his or her own language as well as be able to do so in Spanish. The starting point is the native language. Moreover, this has been the point where traditionally the barrier has been placed—that is, the myth of the insurmountable problem of selecting or developing an alphabet for teaching Guaraní in the schools—which makes bilingual education programs an impossibility. When it appeared that this obstacle had been overcome, it was decided not to release the results of the tests. The program was disbanded. In fact, in a contract signed by AID and the MOE on September 20, 1978, it was agreed that "There will be no effort to teach reading or writing in Guaraní" in the nation's primary schools.

This unfortunate but understandable conclusion to the project may have been foreshadowed by a statement by Jack Barry, who wrote: ". . . an alphabet is successful in so far and only so far as it is scientifically and socially acceptable. The two interests often conflict and it would be a fallacy to assume . . . that the choice of an orthography can be determined solely on grounds that are linguistically or pedagogically desirable" (Barry 1958:752–53). Although it would be pleasant to be able to say that this situation has changed, in reality it remains the same as it was over twenty years ago when Barry first described it. This is demonstrated clearly by the Paraguayan case.

NOTE

Research for this study was carried out in 1977 under a contract with USAID/Paraguay (#526–416). Results of the orthography tests were presented in a report to the agency (Stark 1977*b*). I am grateful for permission to republish parts of the data included in that account. Any conclusions are my own and do not reflect the attitudes or opinions of those either now or previously employed by USAID.

Bilingual Education in Bolivia

Lucy Therina Briggs

A multilingual country without a national bilingual education policy, Bolivia has a population of approximately six million divided among speakers of Spanish, Quechua, and Aymara, as well as some twenty-six minority languages. It is generally conceded that speakers of Quechua and Aymara, taken together, constitute over 60 percent of the population. They live primarily in the western highlands, engaged in agriculture, trade, and mining. The Bolivian sociolinguist Javier Albó points out that 1976 census figures must be revised upward for speakers of vernacular languages and downward for Spanish, to adjust for the fact that Spanish is the prestige language while the others are stigmatized (Albó 1980). Comparison of language statistics from the 1950 and 1976 censuses shows that knowledge of Spanish is increasing, with increasing bilingualism—that is, more speakers of Quechua and Aymara are now able to use Spanish to some extent without having given up their native languages. Nevertheless, Albó sounds a somber note, pointing out that if present trends continue, disappearance of vernacular languages is inevitable though not imminent. While universal Spanish-language acquisition would be of undoubted benefit to the country, must it be achieved at the loss of native languages and cultures?

The tacit answer given to that question by the traditional education system of Bolivia has been yes. The system makes no provision for teaching children in the elementary grades in any language other than Spanish. Article 115 of Chapter X of the Bolivian Code of Education, based on Decree Law 03937 of 1950, refers to the use of vernacular languages in adult literacy programs only, stating merely that native languages will be used "as a vehicle for the im-

mediate learning of Spanish," for which purpose "phonetic alphabets that maintain the greatest possible similarity to the Spanish
alphabet will be adopted" (República de Bolivia 1980:31). Vernacular languages are thus seen as, at best, a bridge to Spanish and,
at worst, a barrier to learning. Children who arrive at school speaking only a vernacular language are taught to "read" Spanish before
they understand what it means. Not surprisingly, dropout rates in
rural schools in areas where the home language is not Spanish are
very high, even when teachers are themselves speakers of the child's
home language, which is not always the case. As noted by contemporary researchers like Skutnabb-Kangas (1979) and Cummins
(1979), the kind of bilingualism attained by children who speak a
low-prestige language at home is often of a subtractive rather than
an additive variety—that is, given no opportunity to develop school
skills in the stigmatized native language, they also fail to attain
educated native-speaker levels in the second language. The result
in Bolivia is very low school achievement and functional illiteracy
for a third of the population. In other words, while 1976 census
figures show increasing bilingualism under the present educational
system, much of it is merely incipient, nonfunctional bilingualism
with functional illiteracy.

BILINGUAL EDUCATION IN THE BOLIVIAN LOWLANDS

Bilingual education in the modern sense of the term was introduced to Bolivia about twenty-five years ago by missionary linguists associated with the Summer Institute of Linguistics (SIL;
known in Spanish-speaking countries as the Instituto Lingüístico de
Verano). In each host country, SIL works through the government,
coordinating its programs with those already in existence (if any).
Bilingual education is an outgrowth of the primary objective of SIL:
the translation of the Bible into all the languages of the world. In
Bolivia, SIL efforts have focused on the minority languages in lowland areas where Spanish is the majority language. SIL linguists
have written grammars and literacy materials, training native speakers
as teachers and supervising the use of the materials in schools.

In November 1980 I was invited to visit two primary schools for Ese Ejja and Cavineña speakers, taught by native speakers of the languages who had been trained as teachers by SIL. Each school was multigrade, with about fifteen children ranging in age from five to twelve. The children read fluently in the native language, were learning to speak and read Spanish, and were able to do accurate arithmetic.

SIL will phase out of Bolivia in the next five years, leaving uncertain the future of the bilingual schools it has started. Once SIL leaves, the schools will probably again be assigned teachers who have no knowledge of the local languages, much less of bilingual education, even though they may have normal school degrees the others lack. Critics of SIL fault that organization for failing to provide training in linguistics to native speakers of the languages studied, and allege that the primary purpose of SIL is not conducive to developing community initiative sufficient to carry on where SIL leaves off. The fact remains that SIL has provided literacy skills and materials in previously unwritten languages in many parts of the world, and its years of experience should be studied by anyone interested in the field of bilingual education. (A group of German anthropological linguists has worked among the Guaraní-speaking Chiriguano in southeastern Bolivia, and report [Schuchard 1979] on the need for bilingual education among them.)

BILINGUAL EDUCATION IN THE HIGHLAND AREAS

Secular efforts in bilingual education have focused on the two majority language groups in the highlands: Quechua and Aymara. Two separate projects undertaken in 1977 under the auspices of the Bolivian government and international funding agencies were designed to experiment with pilot projects in bilingual education. These are a Quechua/Spanish project in Cochabamba and an Aymara/Spanish project in La Paz.

The Quechua/Spanish project is a component of Rural Education Project I, funded by USAID under an agreement with the Bolivian Ministry of Education and administered through a technical assistance contract with the University of New Mexico, in twenty-two rural school districts in the department of Cochabamba. Like SIL, the project uses a transitional model designed to transfer children to all-Spanish classrooms by fourth grade. Information on the project may be found in two reports by USAID consultants (Development Associates, Inc. 1979, 1980) and in Solá and Weber (1978).

The materials developed for the Quechua project resemble commercially published children's books in their use of illustrations in color rather than in black and white, as in the simpler SIL format. The method of teaching reading, beginning with whole words the children already know, is similar to that used by SIL. Materials reflect the structure of Quechua, using a question-and-answer format familiar to the children from riddles and manipulating roots and suffixes in ways they already control orally. (In my opinion, the method could profitably be adapted to teaching reading in Aymara.) Another positive feature is the use of three vowels to write Quechua, which has only three vowel phonemes (as does Aymara). Spelling in Aymara and Quechua is not yet standardized in Bolivia. A controversy exists as to whether it is better to write the two languages with three or five vowels, proponents of five arguing that the allophones [e] and [o] are predictable and therefore that writing them will pose no problems for the beginning reader and will, rather, facilitate eventual transfer of reading skills to Spanish, a five-vowel language. My observations support those of Martin-Barber (1975) and Pyle (1981) to the effect that the allophones are not predictable, and the fact that Aymara and Quechua make only three vowel distinctions argues against using five in writing them, especially in beginning stages of reading.

Technical assistance and loan funding for all components of Rural Education Project I were to end in April 1981, and it was believed that the Ministry of Education would probably not continue to support the bilingual education component of the project. This would be unfortunate, as it has only recently begun to show results. An unedited videotape made in one of the project schools shows children in a bilingual classroom reading easily in both Quechua and Spanish, and answering questions about what they have read, in contrast to children in a traditional classroom—bored and silent—and an older student reading Spanish in the halting manner taught traditionally. According to USAID, lower dropout rates have resulted from the project. Opinions expressed by principals, teachers, and parents are mixed. While an analysis conducted by a Bolivian consulting firm in July 1980 (Rivera et al. 1980) revealed generally favorable attitudes toward the project, an internal evaluation carried out later by Bolivian technicians (Angulo Gallinate et al. 1980) found mainly unfavorable attitudes. A USAID official has observed that support varied depending on the language-use situation in each community, being stronger in Quechua-dominant, and weaker in Spanish-dominant, areas (Dr. Jean Meadowcroft, personal communication).

Persons reported as having unfavorable attitudes said they had received insufficient training in, or information on, the bilingual education methods developed for the project. In support of bilingual education training, in 1980 another USAID project, Rural Education Project II, included such training in a long-term course for rural normal school instructors at the Instituto Superior de Educación in Tarija. The training was provided by three Bolivian instructors who had studied applied linguistics and bilingual education in Colombia under project auspices.

In mid-1980, USAID was planning to expand the Quechua/Spanish bilingual education project to seventy-five rural school districts in Cochabamba and Chuquisaca, but, owing to the great reduction in USAID programs in Bolivia following the July 1980 coup d'état, this project has been indefinitely postponed. After initial research on dialectal variation and child acquisition of syntax in both Spanish and Quechua, the project was to embark on a maintenance bilingual education program starting in kindergarten and continuing through fifth grade. (Maintenance bilingual education maintains and develops children's skills in the native language in addition to teaching them a second language.) The project would stress teacher training, disseminate information on bilingual education to parents and the general public, provide opportunities for parents and community leaders to participate in the program, and produce expendable curriculum materials on a large scale. It would develop basic oral and literacy skills in Quechua with high levels of comprehension and critical reading skills, and introduce Spanish as a second language orally, delaying the introduction of Spanish reading until students have "some oral language background in Spanish . . . and . . . an independent reading ability in Quechua" (Development Associates, Inc. 1980:50).

In its major outlines, the project appears well designed, but in my opinion it fails to take sufficient account of Bolivian sociopolitical realities. As a precondition for a U.S. loan, the project would require the creation of a Department of Bilingual Education that would "help create a national superstructure for the development of bilingual programs." While centralizing and coordinating bilingual education efforts is a laudable objective, it is questionable that the creation of a new government agency would in and of itself attain that objective, given the present lack of support of bilingual education among Bolivian political leaders.

According to Albó (1980:17), the Quechua of Cochabamba is mixed with Spanish to the point that some call it Quechuañol; and there is another mixed dialect in a part of Chuquisaca, called Llapuni for two Quechua suffixes, that reportedly consists of Spanish with Quechua suffixes (ACLO 1972: Ch. 8, cited in Albó 1980:24). Reports such as these call for sociolinguistic analysis to determine the linguistic realities. One project that takes this kind of language situation into account is a small effort in one school sponsored by the Centro Pedagógico y Cultural de Portales in rural Cochabamba, with funds from the Patiño Foundation, a private entity based in Switzerland. For children whose native language is Spanish heavily influenced by Quechua, this project uses a language-experience approach whereby the children's own words and stories are used as the basis for primers. Children learn to read their own dialect, and are then taught a more standard variety of Spanish (and also of Quechua) orally, by a method I have called "progressive differentiation" in another context (Briggs 1982) after a method described by Rubin (1977:292). There appears to have been no formal evaluation of this project as yet.

The Aymara/Spanish counterpart of the bilingual education component of Rural Education Project I was the bilingual education component of the Proyecto Educativo Integrado del Altiplano (PEIA).

Supported by a loan from the World Bank administered through the Ministry of Education, the PEIA was launched in 1977 to improve education of Aymara-speaking children in rural La Paz department through construction of new schools and teacher housing, development of new methods and materials, and teacher training. As originally conceived, the project was to introduce bilingual education with radio support in all the primary schools in the project, serving approximately thirty-eight thousand students. A non-Bolivian specialist in bilingual education was to have been assigned to the project in 1978 to help design and implement the bilingual education plan. By the time I was finally hired, in the fall of 1979, an experiment was already underway in fifteen schools in four provinces of La Paz department, but it turned out to be short-lived.

Unlike the other bilingual education efforts discussed in this article, the PEIA experiment was designed and undertaken by persons who had only minimal, if any, preparation in bilingual education. With hindsight, it would have been preferable to have unified the planning and administration of this project with the bilingual education component of Rural Education Project I in Cochabamba, as had originally been contemplated in 1975 (Consejo de Racionalización Administrativa and Academia para el Desarrollo Educativo 1975). As it was, the PEIA experiment was deficient in several important respects. The method was ostensibly transitional over a three-year period, but during the brief life of the experiment—about ten months in 1979—materials were developed for only the first grade and applied in only fifteen schools. The materials introduced Spanish letters and words in the primer, interspersed with Aymara, in the first few weeks of instruction. The method made no distinction between teaching children to read and teaching Spanish (two different skills) and no provision for teaching Spanish as a second language beyond a tacit acceptance of the common practice, among Aymara-speaking teachers, of translating orally from one language to the other. The methods and materials were developed by a veteran rural teacher, with experience primarily in Quechua-speaking areas, who spoke a variety of Aymara used in Oruro but not in La Paz. He was assisted by two younger rural teachers who were native speakers of La Paz Aymara and who received training in giving the radio lessons that were to complement classroom activities.

Shortly after my arrival at the project in September 1979, I visited a few of the schools where the method was being applied in the first grade. Such visits were soon suspended, however, because of antagonism toward the PEIA stemming from delays in promised school construction. The November coup d'état was also a factor. The results of a survey of participating teachers and of written tests given the students subsequently disappeared from the PEIA files, perhaps because they were largely negative. In February 1980, after months of stagnation, the PEIA underwent a general reorganization spearheaded by a confederation of rural teachers determined to gain control of its operations. The three-man bilingual education team was dismissed from the project along with most of the staff.

The new team of technicians hired for the PEIA in March 1980 consisted mainly of rural Aymara-speaking teachers, most of them young and open to educational innovation. One of them decided to specialize in bilingual education. Following a decision made by the project staff as a whole to conduct an evaluation of the bilingual education experiment, we worked together with the PEIA's consultant in evaluation, also a native speaker of Aymara, to develop a questionnaire and tests to administer to the teachers and children involved in the experiment in 1979 and to other educators and parents familiar with it. These efforts were hampered by the facts that of the total of sixteen teachers (two in one school) who had participated, only five were still teaching the same students, and that these students were now all in second grade in traditional all-Spanish classrooms.

Our evaluation, completed in October 1980 (Mamani et al. 1980), concluded that while the results of the program were poor, it was not a total failure and, indeed, had some positive aspects. The sample of teachers and parents interviewed, on being informed that the goal of bilingual education was literacy and proficiency in both the first and second languages, were disposed to continue the experiment after necessary adjustments and improvements. Children whose teachers had shown interest and enthusiasm in applying the method had learned to read and write to some extent in both Aymara and Spanish, if generally with many errors, especially in spelling. The cultural content of the primers came in for some criticism—for example, the use of the word *achacu* 'mouse' as the first word in the primer. Children were taught to sing a little song (translated from Spanish) that went, "We are mice, we like to eat cheese." The identification of children with a thieving animal that steals human food is culturally unacceptable to rural Aymara, and may help explain why some parents were reportedly resistant to the idea of bilingual education. (To avoid such pitfalls, developers of materials should seek out and incorporate the views of parents and other community leaders in early stages of project development.) Finally, the evaluation noted a general lack of information on file, both as to criteria for selection of schools and teachers and as to planning. Except for one of the radio technicians, none of the persons involved in the planning and execution of the bilingual education experiment was available to provide any additional information.

The evaluation recommended that the bilingual education experiment be continued with different materials and methods, to be developed by a multidisciplinary team on the basis of a survey, of both children and adults, of language patterns and usage in the community. Information on bilingual education would continue to be disseminated to parents and community leaders, and teachers would be trained in the new methods.

In mid-1980, the PEIA technician interested in specializing in bilingual education began to design new materials, including a primer starting with the word *utasa* 'our house', a much more culturally appropriate beginning than *achacu* and a word whose structure— root *uta* plus suffix *-sa*—permitted natural alternation of parts to form new words. During the midwinter vacation in early July, he and I conducted a one-week workshop on bilingual education for rural teachers, with the participation of university professors as lecturers. Several of the thirty-five teachers who regularly attended decided at the end of the workshop to form an organization of teachers interested in bilingual education, to be called Centro Nacional de Investigación y Educación Bilingüe.

Following the coup d'état of mid-July, however, the PEIA underwent yet another reorganization. The technician who wanted to specialize in bilingual education lost his job, and my one-year contract ended. As of this writing, the chances that the PEIA will resume a bilingual education experiment are slim, and will remain so unless project decision makers and their superiors in the Ministry of Education change their views on bilingual education. The general attitude is that children must be *castellanizados* (hispanicized) as quickly as possible by submersion in an all-Spanish program.

OTHER EFFORTS RELATED TO DEVELOPMENTS IN BILINGUAL EDUCATION

Contrasting with officially sponsored projects are the individual efforts of a few rural teachers, bilingual in Aymara and Spanish, who teach reading and writing in Aymara using a phonemic three-vowel alphabet adopted by the University of San Andrés in La Paz for teaching Aymara as a second language. One teacher has reported that older, nonreading students learned to read for the first time when given materials in Aymara (Copana:1981). Once having understood that reading involves decoding meaning, they were able within a very short time to transfer the skill of reading to Spanish, which they could already speak to some extent. Individual efforts such as this merit careful study and evaluation.

Aymara teachers are given moral support by the privately funded Instituto de Lengua y Cultura Aymara, which sponsors the collection, transcription, and publication of materials in Aymara. In 1980, pamphlet-style primers focusing on the family and farm animals (Yapita 1979) were distributed free to elementary schoolteachers, and a detailed history of Aymara alphabets written by a rural teacher was published (Layme 1980). The Instituto Nacional de Estudios Lingüísticos, a dependency of the Ministry of Education, publishes materials useful for teacher training in bilingual education, such as a contrastive study of Aymara and Spanish phonology (Boynton 1980) and a survey of Aymara/Quechua/Spanish trilingualism in northern Potosí (Hosokawa 1980). (For additional information on Aymara publications, see Briggs 1979.)

The involvement of the University of San Andrés in bilingual education merits special mention. In early 1980, through the joint efforts of the then director of the Linguistics Program, Professor José Mendoza, and instructors of Aymara and Quechua, as well as the initiative of a group of young rural teachers (many of them on the staff of the PEIA), a special program leading toward the *Licenciatura* (master's) in education, with a focus on bilingual education, was established for teachers. Unfortunately, the program was abruptly suspended when the university was closed following the July 1980 coup d'état, and not resumed until 1982, on a reduced scale.

CONCLUSIONS

In the absence of a national bilingual education policy, a practical approach in Bolivia today would be to develop a few modest experiments with the active participation of teachers and community leaders who are native speakers of the vernacular languages concerned. The focus should be on teacher training and development of materials with the aid of community members (see, for example, Wigginton 1975) in a team approach designed to enhance the skills of Bolivian nationals. Different models of instruction (transitional, maintenance, and teaching directly in the second language) could be tried and compared with the traditional model, and methods devised to deal with the multigrade classroom. Evaluation should be continuous, and should include ethnographic and linguistic analyses of the classroom (cf. McDermott 1977).

To prepare the way for eventual resumption of larger-scale efforts, a high priority should be given to disseminating articles and books in Spanish that describe bilingual education experiences relevant to the Bolivian situation, such as those in Peru and Mexico (see Troike and Modiano 1975; Sánchez Garrafa and Riedmiller 1980; Solá and Weber 1978; and Larson, Davis, and Ballena Dávila 1979). Another prerequisite for large-scale efforts is teacher training, especially in methods of teaching reading in the native language and methods of teaching Spanish as a second language. Teachers should be prepared to explain the benefits of bilingual education to parents, without whose support no program can succeed. I found parents to be very supportive of bilingual education when they understood its objectives. Decision makers would also be supportive if they understood the rationale for bilingual educa-

tion. It is up to those of us who do understand it to present the
evidence in ways too clear to be ignored.

NOTE

I wish to thank Dr. Jean Meadowcroft of USAID/Bolivia for commenting on an earlier draft of this article and providing information on USAID
programs. The interpretations of the data are my own.

Social Stratification and Implications for Bilingual Education: An Ecuadorian Example

LAWRENCE K. CARPENTER

One of the general goals of most bilingual education programs is to aid and benefit a linguistic minority within a larger society. Moreover, it often is believed by the educational bureaucracy that the merits of bilingual education will help convince the target population of the program's value and consequently increase the desire of the linguistic minority to broaden its participation in formal education. However, these basic goals are usually defined and incorporated at an administrative level far above and beyond the participation of local community leaders. As a result, the myth of minority homogeneity is perpetuated and inadvertently included in the design and realization of the bilingual program. The interplay of factors surrounding the Ecuadorian National Plan of Bilingual Education is used in this paper to illustrate some of the problems encountered by administratively initiated projects.

Following the recommendations of the Primer Seminario Nacional de Educación Bilingüe (PSNEB) held in Quito in 1973, Ecuador has initiated a national policy of bilingual education to address the ". . . urgent necessity of sociocultural and economic integration. . . ." of the linguistic minorities in the country (PSNEB 1975). Although Spanish is the official language, Ecuador is a linguistically diverse nation. The majority of the population of seven million speak at least one of ten indigenous languages. Quichua, which is further subdivided into at least thirteen dialects, is the most widely spoken of the indigenous languages.

Almost a decade after the Primer Seminario, to the bewilderment of educators and government policy makers, it has been found that not all programs are well received or successful, even though the merits of bilingual education in Ecuador have been demonstrated by social scientists. (See Dilworth and Stark 1975; Carpenter 1974.) Even within a single ethnic group that is favorably disposed toward bilingual education, not all members feel it to be a viable alternative to the existing system of education with instruction in Spanish. When educators and policy makers become aware of the disparate desires of a given ethnic group regarding bilingual education, the following questions often arise. What are the factors that help determine the decision of minority members to participate or not to participate in bilingual programs? And are such factors cultural, linguistic, or a combination—that is, sociolinguistic? By examining in this article certain linguistic and cultural data from the Otavalo Indians, I propose to describe some of these defining characteristics, their interaction, and their effect on the acceptance or rejection of proposed bilingual education programs.

CULTURAL CONSIDERATIONS

The Otavaleños are an indigenous group of about forty thousand people residing in the higher valleys of the Imbabura Province in northern Ecuador. In addition, expatriate enclaves exist in New York, Madrid, Bogotá, and Rio de Janeiro. While the majority of this ethnic group are still subsistence agriculturalists, approximately 20 percent are intensively engaged in a primarily tourist-oriented production weaving economy. Because of this latter group's wide dispersion in Ecuador and abroad and their involvement with the tourist industry, the Otavaleños are becoming increasingly known.

An element contributing to this growing visibility is the Otavalo Saturday-morning market, one of Ecuador's major tourist attractions as well as one of the most famous artisan markets in South America. For the local residents the Saturday market itself is generally the focal point of the week, and much of the town's activities are oriented toward it.

The market has become so well known that even a three-day tour of Ecuador usually will include a trip to Otavalo. If a tour does not coincide with market day, visitors are taken to one of the smaller outlying communities surrounding Otavalo, where the inhabitants are well aware of the economic benefits of tourism. Upon the imminent arrival of a tour group, a normally quiet plaza is quickly and seemingly spontaneously filled with all the hustle and bustle of a regular Saturday market. As quickly as it began, this apparently impromptu market activity disappears with the departure of the tour group, and the inhabitants resume their normal daily routines.

Several factors have contributed to the prominence of the market as a major tourist attraction and source of income. Unlike the situation in the Andean region farther south, where weavings are generally for personal use, substantial quantities of the textiles produced by the Otavaleños are primarily for selling in the tourist market. Such production weaving has long been a part of the Otavalo society. Within a year of the Spanish Conquest, land was being granted to the new settlers, and Otavalo became part of a large encomienda given to Rodrigo de Salazar. By the 1550s, Salazar had initiated a large weaving *obraje* in the area, which consisted of as many as five hundred workers at the height of its productivity (Casagrande 1977). As Salomon (1973) indicated, the Spanish succeeded in expanding weaving from a ". . . local craft to an export industry . . . ," and, as such, the Otavalo area produced a large portion of the textiles utilized in colonial South America. Within this century, *kashimir* (tweed) woven by the Otavaleños further increased demands for their skills and services. By the time tweed fell out of fashion, Otavalo had been established as a place where good, durable textiles could be bought.

As the fame of Otavalo increased—with its subsequent economic benefits—the market, the town, and interethnic relations also changed. A physical change in the market was instigated by the Dutch government in the early 1970s with the construction of cement kiosks where the Otavaleños could sell their work, theoretically making the products more appealing to foreign tourists than weavings displayed on the ground. The operating hours also changed. In the early 1970s, the market usually closed between 9:00 and 10:00 A.M., whereas the present-day market continues until the early afternoon. As one Indian explained, "We've learned that you gringos don't like to get up early, so the market is longer now."

Changes in the town can be illustrated by the shifting Indian/ blanco proportion within the urban population. In the 1940s, Otavalo was referred to as "the world of the white man; the Indians enter it with distrust and leave it gladly for the peace and oldness of the mountains" (Collier and Buitrón 1949). There were very few Indians in residence in the town itself. Within the past four decades, however, increasing numbers of Indians have taken up residence in Otavalo, thereby becoming city Indians. Today there are approximately three thousand Indians among the twelve thousand inhabitants of Otavalo. Many of the Indians remaining in the countryside do not approve of this urban migration, and refer to their city-dwelling counterparts by saying that they have "forgotten their origin in the land, . . . are lazy . . . and . . . are soft like little leaves." Although rural Indians generally disapprove of living in the city, many share the desire for material possessions, and say that "there is a treasure that shines only for those in the city."

Most urban Indians own or rent homes and stores, especially in the north end of town near the tourist market. This Indian settlement pattern, resulting from rural to urban migration, has brought new types of business to the urban area. There are at least seventy-five stores selling *artesanía*, most of them Indian-owned and -operated; in 1966, the same area contained a single, white-owned shop.

As an example of the intricacies of interethnic relations, the interdependency of various social groups can be illustrated by the appearance of wool sweaters in the market. An early Peace Corps project introduced knitting to the non-Indian women of a more northern community. Many of these women buy much of their wool from the Otavaleños, knit the sweaters, then sell them back to the Otavaleños, who in turn sell them to tourists and other buyers. When asked why the women do not sell the sweaters themselves, one woman explained, "We make them and the Indians sell them; people like to buy from the Indians, not from us." All involved seem to be quite happy with this arrangement. Many of the women now have new homes, and the Otavaleños have another highly salable item in their textile inventory.

Because being recognized as Otavaleño is seen as an economic advantage, some Indians who normally wear non-Indian clothing during the week appear at the Saturday market in full Indian costume. Even some white people wear Indian costumes on Saturday in an effort to attract more business.

The growth of the weaving industry and the market has increased considerably the economic independence and visibility of those Otavaleños most closely associated with it. However, the farther one goes from the market into the countryside, the more economic benefits decline. Along with other factors, such as residence, religion, amount of education, and socialization of the youngest child, this increased economic viability has caused the emergence of a new social class that is relatively wealthy and that sometimes has considerable influence among the other Otavaleños. The following examples demonstrate the degree of wealth manifested. Whenever possible, the Otavaleños purchase land but, beyond this, seem to be very taken by the products of more technologically advanced societies. Many of the wealthy merchants in the Saturday market own pocket calculators. One man has a pocket translator to facilitate interaction with English-speaking clients. Within the Indian home, it is not unusual to see refrigerators, blenders, stoves, color TV sets, expensive stereo sound systems, and electric looms. (These looms are turned off on Saturdays, so that the tourists will not suspect machine production.) Since the cost of these imported items is at least double that in the exporting country, their acquisition involves a substantial outlay of capital.

Investigations by Stark (n.d.), Villavicencio (1973), Burgos (1977), and others have addressed the phenomena of social stratification and interethnic relations within the broader context of Ecuadorian society. Other investigations (see, for example, Chavez 1979) have shown that, in addition to occupying certain social positions as a group within the larger society, the Otavaleños are further experiencing in-group class distinctions.

Beyond economic differences, some of the more salient social characteristics of the emerging upwardly mobile class of Indians are as follows. (1) *Residence*. As stated earlier, most of the members of this new social class reside within the town of Otavalo or in expatriate communities. Furthermore, most of these people are from the nearby communities of Peguche, Quinchuquí, Ilumán, and Agato. (2) *Religion*. Many, although not all, of the urban Indians have converted from Catholicism and now are either *evangélicos* or *ad-ventistas*. (3) *Costume*. Until about forty years ago, slight varia-tions in dress indicated the area or community of residence. Variations in the hat styles, blouse, belt design, *anaku* (skirt) embroidery, and the *fachalina* (head wrap) in different combinations helped to iden-tify clearly the village of residence. Today, most of these local var-iants have largely disappeared owing to the increasing specialization in the costume manufacture. Although it is still possible within lim-its to determine residence from certain costume elements like the *walka* (neck beads), the more recent economy and subsequent in-troduction of new fabrics have caused former distinctions based on residence to now be distinctions based primarily on wealth and sta-tus. For example, among women, wearing an anaku, fachalina, or *rebozo* (carrying cloth of velvet, velour, or fake fur) is indicative more of social class than of residence. Among men, social position and wealth are often indicated by tailor-made pants, digital watches, sunglasses, racing jackets instead of ponchos, not wearing hats, and, occasionally among the youth, Nike running shoes and de-signer jeans.

LINGUISTIC CONSIDERATIONS

Because social change is usually followed by language change, one can expect to find linguistic variation reflecting the new social stratification. As Labov (1966) pointed out in his seminal work, any social distinction based on nonlinguistic criteria may nonetheless be mirrored by linguistic variation. Indeed, many recent innova-tions in language use and attitudes among the Otavaleños support this claim.

Although not always the case, a majority of the Otavaleños cur-rently speak Quichua, a member of the Quechua language family. The Otavaleños were the last group to be brought under the yoke of Inca domination during Huayna Capac's northern campaign. After a fierce seventeen-year resistance, the Otavaleños finally yielded to the Incas, and were ruled by them for a short time before the arrival of the Spanish in 1534. As was customary, the Incas attempted to impose their language, religion, and other customs on the Otavaleños, but apparently with little success. In a 1582 description, Sancho Paz Ponce de León stated that there were "many languages different one from the other [varieties of Cara] and different from that of the Inca [Quechua]" (1964:9; my translation and interpretation). Although the use of Cara probably continued until well after the Conquest, almost nothing remains today but toponyms. The replacement of Cara by Quichua is so complete that most of the present-day Otavaleños are monolingual Quichua speakers. However, the closer one gets to the town of Otavalo, the higher the incidence of Quichua/Spanish bilingualism.

The various ethnic groups in Ecuador have distinct ways of referring to the Quichua language, such as *runa shimi* (Indian/human language), *inga shimi* (Inca language), or *inga parlu* (Inca speech). However, the Otavaleños are unique in referring to their language as *yanga shimi*. In the early 1970s, everyone I asked said this meant "a worthless language." During my last field trip, the majority of the rural inhabitants still defined the term this way, but many of the urban inhabitants said the term meant "independent" or "segregated language." This lexical change reflects a growing appreciation by the Indians of the importance of the language to their ethnic identity.

A grammatical change paralleling the above is the difference between the rural and urban speakers regarding distinctions in the pronoun system. The urban group distinguishes between curved/polite and straight/abrupt second-person pronouns *kikin* and *kan*, respectively. The rural population and the other ethnic groups in Ecuador generally maintain kan as the only second-person referent.

While many variations of Otavalo Quichua are indicative of the urban/rural distinctions in social dialectology, others illustrate stylistic, age, sex, and/or social network distinctions as well. For example, older women use the more conservative form *ñuñukuy* (to put in the blouse) instead of the innovative form *jinchuliy* (to put in the blouse). The latter is more widespread among the younger women in addition to being the more prevalent form among urban women. In addition to social dialects, geographic dialectology exists both inter- and intragroup, but is beyond the scope of the present article. (See Stark and Carpenter [1974] for major subdialect distributions within the Otavalo dialect.)

As an example of an age indicator regardless of sex, consider the

Quichua forms meaning "to dance." *Baylana*, from Spanish *bailar*, is by far the most general term. The urban young, after the appearance of the film *Saturday Night Fever*, have created *trabultiyana*, via Spanish *travoltear* from English (John) Travolta. As an indicator of religious affiliation regardless of age and sex, the non-Catholics, many of them urban, have reborrowed the more conservative *tushuna* from Peruvian Quechua meaning "to dance."

When referring to *wagra* (cow), people involved in cattle rustling generally use the term *ankara* (large gourd bottom). The similarity of the large gourd bottom with the cow's head with its horns is illustrative of this group's euphemistic reference to items by their shape, thereby maintaining privacy in their public conversations.

Although these examples are not an exhaustive description of the variation in Otavalo social dialectology, they are indicative of some of the major distinctions.

SOCIOLINGUISTIC CONSIDERATIONS

The cultural and linguistic elements presented above are not the only factors indicative of the ongoing social stratification process in Otavalo. An extremely important sociolinguistic consideration is the evaluation of the differences between the attitudes toward, and perceptions of, Spanish, Quichua, and bilingual education by the rural poor and the urban wealthy. Once these differences are perceived, the acceptability of introduced bilingual programs can be enhanced by corresponding differences in program presentation and composition addressing the needs of specific groups.

Among the urban wealthy, some of the younger generation are in the process of losing their Quichua. Many adolescents understand Quichua, but prefer to speak Spanish, claiming that the former language causes their ". . . tongues to get twisted. . . ." Many preadolescents are now Spanish-speaking monolinguals. This does not mean that Quichua is moribund among the Indians. The vast majority of the Otavaleños still have Quichua as their native language. Among the urban inhabitants, the parents do not want their children to lose the ability to speak Quichua since it is now becoming an important element in their ethnic identity. While they feel that Spanish is more useful in their business affairs, Quichua is still the language of their rural home, jokes, ceremonies, and medicine. For many of these people, bilingual education is seen as a way to prevent the loss of the indigenous language.

On the other hand, the often monolingual rural poor see the acquisition of Spanish as necessary for economic advancement, social mobility, and the acquisition of material wealth. They usually perceive bilingual education as an attempt to keep them predominantly Quichua speakers and to deny them access to the wealth and status of their urban counterparts. Their feeling is that, since their children already know Quichua, they must go to school in Spanish in order to force them to learn that language. The following quote from one of my informants is representative of this point of view. "This is usually what happened in the public schools; almost nothing is written in Quichua, so why on earth would anyone want to learn to read and write that language? Anything to be read is in Spanish, and anything worth writing about will also be in that language."

Many proponents of bilingual education will argue that reading and writing skills in Quichua will enable the Indian population to prepare important documents, such as deeds and wills, in their native language. Unfortunately, this is not now considered socially acceptable by the Indians or legally acceptable by the Ecuadorian government.

In addition to these language-related concerns, the origins of bilingual education in Ecuador help contribute to its rejection or acceptance at the local level. Much of the present interest in bilingual education stems from the impetus of such international development agencies as the Summer Institute of Linguistics, Peace Corps, and AID. Adopted at the government level by the political and economic elite as a possible solution to the "Indian problem," various pilot projects of bilingual education appeared at the regional and local levels. Almost all projects were (and are) transitional—that is, moving from the use of Quichua to predominantly Spanish-speaking bilingualism. It was hoped that such programs would help the economic, social, and political integration of Indians into Ecuadorian life. In many regions, the upwardly mobile opt for bilingual education, while those who are proud of their Indian identity often reject it. In the Otavalo region, the majority of the rural Quichua-speaking population perceive bilingual education as yet another mechanism of repression designed to perpetuate their poverty and servitude. The urban Indian population perceive bilingual education as a way of maintaining the Quichua language, so important to ethnic identity, and not as a way of integration. It appears that somewhere between the inception of bilingual education in the centralized administrative offices of the capital and its presentation to the local community, the explanation of its goals and principles seems to have been forgotten. As one Indian explained, "Why would I want to become part of the mainstream of Ecuadorian life; we have our own culture . . . and when we can learn Spanish, you can see that we often do better than many of the non-Indians who live here."

CONCLUSIONS

In the above discussion, cultural, linguistic, and sociolinguistic evidence was presented as illustrative of emerging indicators and markers in the current social stratification process among the Otavaleños. Culturally, membership in a given social class can be determined by residence (rural/urban), costume (composition/materials), religious affiliation (Catholic/non-Catholic), employment (agriculture/weaving), economic status (wealthy/poor), and other factors in varying combinations. Linguistically, social class memberships can be determined by the use of certain lexical items and grammatical forms. Sociolinguistically, class membership can be defined by attitudes toward, and perceptions of, Spanish and Quichua.

It is clear that social stratification among the Otavaleños is occurring, and that membership within a given class is often a determining factor in the acceptance or rejection of national policies such as bilingual education. Instead of the existence of a presumed homogeneous indigenous population, there are different groups and within these class distinctions based on cultural, linguistic, and sociolinguistic considerations. As illustrated by the Otavalo case, acceptance of, and participation in, bilingual education is not determined by purely linguistic factors but by economic ones as well.

While educators and policy makers may claim that economic considerations should not be the factors that determine acceptance or rejection of bilingual education, the empirical evidence from Otavalo indicates that economic status is in fact one of the major decisive elements. The urban wealthy of Otavalo desire bilingual education, not because their children will retain the indigenous language but because by speaking it they are, in part, recognized as Indian. Such recognition is crucial to further economic success. The rural poor, on the other hand, are predominantly monolingual Quichua speakers who want to learn Spanish to increase the possibility of economic advancement. Bilingual education is often rejected by them because the study of Quichua is not seen as economically beneficial.

Ultimately, for bilingual education to be successful anywhere, the various desires, needs, and cultural, linguistic, and sociolinguistic differences of the target population must be ascertained before program planning can begin. Administrative instigators of bilingual programs must incorporate the concerns of the target population in their design. Unless such efforts are made early in the planning phase, bilingual education may be misunderstood by the target group, viewed by them as yet another means of repression, and, as we have seen so often in the past, doomed to failure from its inception.

NOTE

Field research for this article was carried out under the auspices of the Inter-American Foundation and Fulbright-Hays. I would especially like to thank my comadres and compadres for their patience in helping me understand the ways of the people of the land. Participants at board meetings of the Jatari Foundation, as well as colleagues and professors at the University of Florida, are responsible for stimulating discussions on the topic. Responsibility for errors and interpretations remains with me.

Bilingual Aspects of Language in a Creole Community

Ronald Kephart

One of the traditional measures of academic success in the West Indies has for many years been performance on an external examination such as the Cambridge General Certificate. A "pass" on the English-Language portion of these exams, which until very recently were set and graded in Great Britain, is necessary for any kind of upward mobility in West Indian society—that is, further education or prestigious employment. The number of West Indians who have never passed this exam is overwhelming. For example, in Trinidad and Tobago from 1974 to 1978, only 22 percent of those taking the English-Language "O-Level" exam managed to pass (Republic of Trinidad and Tobago 1978).

There are several reasons for this, including the following. (1) It is a poorly constructed exam. (2) Biased grading ensures that only the number of passes desired by the exam committee will in fact occur. (3) There is a lack of trained teachers in the West Indies, and teaching methods there are often poor. While these factors are important in explaining the low number of passes over the years, I wish to focus on another: although English always has been assumed to be the native language of the population taking the exam, this is in fact not the case. Failure to take this into account has been, and continues to be, a major obstacle to realistic education in the West Indies.

Carriacou is an island in the Grenadines that belongs to Grenada. Population of the island is about six thousand, with many other Carriacouans living in the metropolitan centers of London and New York. (For an excellent ethnographic description, see Hill 1977.) While Carriacou itself is rather small—about twelve square miles in area—the general situation I am about to describe can be applied to most, if not all, of the nominally English-speaking Caribbean. I plan to suggest that Carriacou should be considered a bilingual community, and that it would be useful for Carriacouans and other West Indians to take a close, objective look at their linguistic situation; only in this way can education in these islands really be improved.

For the purpose of this discussion, I wish to posit the term Export English to replace the more usual label Standard English. Export English refers to the idealized, prestige form of English toward which most of the anglophone world aspires. The word export emphasizes the fact that this variety of English usually reaches former colonial areas as an exported item in the form of books, magazines, newspapers, school textbooks, radio broadcasts, and external exams. Export English also reaches the Caribbean by means of people such as tourists, Peace Corps volunteers, missionaries, and expatriates. It must be made clear, however, that these people do not really speak Export English, even though they may think they do and hope that others will perceive them as doing so. Radio announcers and other professional speakers come close to Export English when they are on guard. But there really are no native speakers of Export English. It might be said that Export English is best exemplified by its written form, which is the most idealized and abstract form and the one furthest removed from individual speakers.

The present linguistic situation in Carriacou is the result of three main waves of human migration. First, various American Indian groups, including the Arawak and Carib, moved northward through the Lesser Antilles from mainland South America. These people were mostly destroyed, except for small pockets of resistance, by early contact with Europeans. The arrival of French planters and their West African slaves in the seventeenth century signaled the second wave. Finally, the third wave consisted of English-speaking settlers and their slaves who appeared in the late eighteenth century. All these groups have contributed to present-day language in Carriacou.

From the first wave, a few words for local plants and animals have survived: *maniku* 'opossum', *zandoulii* 'lizard', *tatu* 'armadillo', *zutii* 'nettle' (see Appendix for an explanation of Carriacou

Creole orthography used in this paper). During the second wave, French and probably several West African languages were introduced, as well as an early variety of Creole French (see Brinkley 1978 for a description of Carriacou in 1750). With the third wave, English and some form of English Creole, perhaps similar to Jamaican Creole in its early stages, were brought in. It appears, however, that the second wave of influence has remained very strong. Creole French, locally called *Patwa*, is still spoken by many people. The local variety of Lesser Antillean Creole English (Hancock 1977), called by its speakers *Broukn Inglish* and which I call Carriacou Creole, appears to have been heavily influenced by Creole French phonology. In addition, a number of local plants and animals are known by their *Patwa* names, even by those who do not actually speak *Patwa*—for example, *gwãgozhei* 'pelican'.

To make matters more complex, there exists in Carriacou a local variety of what Craig (1974) has called Standard West Indian English. This is spoken at times by teachers, administrators, bureaucrats, and others aspiring toward Export English. This variety of English seems to be relatively constant throughout the West Indies. Between Standard West Indian English and Carriacou Creole there is an area of variability within which people operate, depending on the situation, the extent of their education, and their exposure to Export English.

Linguistic variation in Carriacou is summarized in Figure 1 (adapted from Craig 1974:372). The arrows in the diagram represent the directions in which linguistic influences generally flow. Hence, for example, Export English influences features of Standard

Figure 1. Language Variation in Carriacou

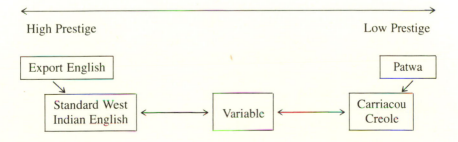

West Indian English, but the reverse is not true. The variable area is marked by the appearance of such Export English forms as the past tense suffix, the possessive suffix, the use of the copula in other than equational/existential constructions, and the dental fricatives.

CARRIACOU AS A BILINGUAL COMMUNITY

The appearance and nonappearance of items like those just mentioned are often accounted for by some kind of deficiency model that assumes that the only grammatical system in operation is that of the standard language, in this case Export English. The missing features are then deleted under certain conditions in the speech of persons who have not attained sufficient mastery of the prestige forms. Previous work (Bailey 1966; Farquhar 1974; Kephart 1980) has shown that it is possible to discover the autonomous structure of various Caribbean Creoles without reference to Export English. The anthropological linguistic field methods I used to analyze Carriacou Creole were identical to those used to discover the structure of such non-Western languages as Bambara and Urhobo-Isoko, both from West Africa—that is to say, these languages at the low-prestige end of the social spectrum are in fact logical, orderly, grammatical, and subject to scientific analysis (see Hardman-de-Bautista and Hamano 1981 for discovery methodology).

Carriacou people have access to the underlying system of Carriacou Creole. This access is not usually conscious. Native speakers of a language rarely are able to state the rules of their grammar unless they have had linguistic training. They can, however, state whether a given sentence is well formed. For example, the suffix *-in* is used in Carriacou Creole to mark an action as in progress at the time being spoken of: *wi ron-in* 'we are/were running'. But consultants always reject sentences like * *wi dei-in* 'we are/were in the process of being (somewhere)' because *dei* 'to be' belongs to a class of verbs that cannot take the incompletive suffix. This argues against the idea, put forth by some observers of West Indian culture, that Creole language is merely a collection of "free-form" idiosyncracies (see, for example, Starbird 1979).

A further illustration, even more revealing, of the access people have to the grammar of Carriacou Creole was found on one of my tapes. I had left the tape recorder with a group of schoolchildren, about fourteen or fifteen years of age, and simply asked them to talk about any subject. Throughout the tape, most of the children chatted un-self-consciously about past experiences. At one point, a usually quiet boy—and good student—began to talk about a crab-hunting expedition; but the others, mostly girls, interrupted him because they felt he was not "speaking bad." I had instructed the children to talk as they normally would in an out-of-school context, and they were taking me quite seriously. In the following sequence transcribed from the tape, the girls instruct the boy in how to get back into Creole grammar.

> Boy: Wan dei tu frenz, may broda an ay went toch-in.
> Girl A: Dou sei dat! Spiik bad! Spiik bad!
> Boy: Wel . . .
> Girl A: Sei "mi broda an mi."
> Girl B: Mi and mi broda.
> Boy: Mi and mi broda . . .
> Girl B: "Wan dei mi an mi broda" sei dat.
> Boy: Wan dei mi an mi broda . . . (laughs) . . . tu ov os an tu oda frenz went toch–in.
> Girl A: Wi di–gou–in an toch.
> Girl B: Mi an mi broda di–gou–in an toch.
> Boy: Oukei. Mi an mi broda di–gou–in an toch.
> Girls: Aa-haa.

It is true that there are at least two self-contained grammatical systems, not just different lexical inventories, present in Carriacou, which leads me to categorize Carriacou as a bilingual community. Although it might be argued that the situation is better described as diglossic, I think the concept of bilingualism makes more sense in this case. In a diglossic situation, there are no native speakers of the prestige language, which is learned by those who wish—or who are allowed—to participate in the activities of the elite class, such as education or government. In a bilingual situation, there are native speakers of both languages, but one enjoys more prestige than the other, usually because it is spoken by those in power. In the case of the British West Indies, which have always maintained close ties with Great Britain, native speakers of varieties of English closest to Export English have had a tremendous influence on the total culture of the native speakers of Creole. More often than not, these people have actually been in control politically and economically. Before independence, governors were usually sent out from Great Britain to manage the affairs of the dependent areas. Until very recently, non-Creole speakers were more likely to be estate owners, heads of schools, or government officials.

The basic difference between this context and other bilingual situations is that in the British West Indies the native speakers of the prestige language are separated from the native speakers of the non-prestige language by a large body of water. In more traditional models, the languages are in closer contact. I maintain that in places like Carriacou geographical proximity is replaced by cultural, economic, and political proximity, which translates as dependence on the metropole.

IMPLICATIONS FOR EDUCATION

The fact that there are so many lexical similarities between Carriacou Creole and Export English has made it easy for educators, planners, and others to overlook or actually to be unaware of the more fundamental differences in the underlying grammatical systems. This fact has important social ramifications. As already mentioned, mastery of English has long been a prerequisite for educational advancement. Those who were, and are, unable to achieve this mastery formed a pool of cheap labor that even after emancipation continued to contribute to the one-sided overdevelopment of the metropole. Those who formed this class assumed, as did the elite, that their inability to become proficient in English was due to their own mental deficiency rather than to the fact that their native language was different from Export English. The ease with which people can be mystified into believing that Creole is nothing more than ungrammatical English meant that no one had to think about teaching English with special foreign-language methods.

The nature of the bilingual problem for education in Carriacou is vividly illustrated by examination of materials intended for the teaching of reading in primary schools, such as *Nelson's New West Indian Readers* (Borely 1978). These were supposedly designed especially to introduce West Indian children to reading. *Infant Book 1* contains ten sentences intended to be read by very young students (Borely 1978:11). All these sentences, of course, contain differences in phonology between Export English and the corresponding Creole forms. But leaving phonology aside, all the sentences except number 7 contain differences at the morphological, lexical, and semantic levels. In number 4, the only problem is the use of "pup" for the more likely Carriacou Creole form *popii*—not a glaring difficulty. But all the other sentences have items that occur in Export English but not in Creole or that, if shared with Creole, have a different semantic value. These are as follows. (1) Export English uses "has" where Creole uses *av*; verb stems are invariant in Creole. (2) Export English uses past tense forms "bit" and "got" where Creole prefers *bayt* and *gyet*. Past tense is not obligatory in Creole. (3) Export English "get" is used in the sense of "go get (something)." The Creole for this is *gou fo*. (4) Export English "is" is used in the locative sense. Carriacou Creole prefers *dei* "to be present (here or there)" in this context.

In Table 1, the ten sentences just discussed are presented as they appear in the *Reader* and as they would likely be spoken by a Carriacouan of five or six years.

Eight of these ten sentences, then, contain items that Carriacouan children either do not have in their basic lexicon (has, got, bit) or that occur in different contexts (is, get). Presumably, for efficient

Table 1. Ten Sentences in Export English and Carriacou Creole

Export English Form	Carriacou Creole Form
1. The dog has a pup.	Di daag av a popii.
2. The boy has a cat.	Di boy av a kyat.
3. Dad has a big pig.	Dad av a big pig.
4. Pat the pup, Dad.	Pat di popii, Dad.
5. The dog bit the cat.	Di daag bayt di kayt.
6. The cat got a big cut.	Di kyat gyet a big kot.
7. Bad dog.	Bad daag.
8. Get the bat, Pat.	Gou fo di bat, Pat.
9. The bat is on the bed.	Di bat dei aan di bed.
10. The pup is on the cot.	Di popii dei aan di kaat.

teaching/learning to take place, the children would have to learn these Export English structures before attempting to read them. A few language-sensitive teachers may realize intuitively what is going on. But for the most part there is simply no awareness—at least at the conscious level—of any legitimate system apart from Export English. It is assumed that children speaking Creole are speaking ungrammatical English. But learning to read in this situation means learning a new grammar and lexicon at the same time, and few children are capable of doing this without special guidance. Those who are capable comprise the few who succeed in school and manage to pass the exams that come later.

There is already a certain amount of informal bilingual education taking place in Carriacou. Teachers, who control more of the variable area between Export English and Creole than do most schoolchildren, sometimes make use of their bilingualism in the classroom. Reading teachers, whose materials are in Export English, sometimes translate stories informally and allow children to answer questions in Creole. However, this is always done orally and usually after the children have failed to understand a passage or question in Export English. Also, teachers sometimes conduct parts of a lesson in Creole to make children more comfortable discussing a potentially embarrassing subject such as sex.

My contention is that if Carriacou children are to learn to read Export English effectively and in greater numbers, bilingual education needs to be formalized. I suggest that Carriacouans be taught to read and write in Creole before they tackle Export English. An alphabet of the kind I have used in this paper could be used for this purpose. Since this orthography is phonemic, it should be easy to learn. But, most important, the children would be reading and writing what they have in their heads, instead of what someone else thinks should be in their heads. Thus the initial exposure to literacy would be more positive, less fraught with failure, and more pleasant for children and teachers as well.

Once literacy is attained in Creole, which ought to take less than one school year, the children could begin to learn Export English. Structures of Export English that differ from Creole could be taught systematically using various foreign-language teaching methods. Most of the Creole orthography I have presented here would be transferable to Export English. A few new associations would have to be learned, but the children already would have a tremendous head start.

Perhaps I should emphasize that the matter of transfer from Creole to Export English is not the central issue here. I believe that what is important is that the children will have had a positive experience with the written word and with their own linguistic system. They will have a chance to explore and play with their own language in the prestigious school context, and they will have the tools to continue doing so even after they learn Export English. For the first time in their history as a linguo-cultural group, they will have the satisfaction of knowing that, in a world that values the printed word above almost everything else, their language can be represented in print. The end result should be people who have established a positive relationship to literacy through their native language and then extended this habit to Export English. (For a discussion of the importance of content in literacy materials and a review of recent research in this field, see Willows, Borwick, and Hayvren 1981.)

Of course, a program such as that proposed will require a great shift in attitude away from the almost universal disparagement of Creole and other "nonstandard" varieties of language. Such changes cannot occur overnight. One North American visiting Carriacou in 1979 told me that she thought Creole should be "wiped out" by taking children away from their parents before they begin to talk and raising them in a "proper" language environment where they could learn to speak "precisely." This same person thought that speaking only Creole caused one's brain cells to deteriorate. This is reminiscent of the dialect-eradication school of thought, an ethnocentric if not racist position that self-proclaimed linguists sometimes propound (for an example of this way of thinking, see Morse 1980).

One of the objections to the proposal I have put forth would likely be that it is too expensive, especially for third-world nations. This objection is founded on the assumption, common in the developed world, that teaching materials have to be slick, glossy, four-color productions of the big publishing houses. In fact, it is possible to produce effective, relatively attractive, and culturally relevant primers and other materials with nothing more than a mimeograph machine, stencils, paper, and the talent available—if not always appreciated—in the school and community at large. I prepared a little photocopied primer for about forty cents; if mimeographed, it would be cheaper still. I like to think of this as "guerrilla education." This little booklet probably is all that would be needed to teach children the orthography I have devised for Carriacou Creole. My own son, who is five and has visited Carriacou with me, colored the pictures and had no trouble learning to sound out the words even though he is not a native speaker of Creole. Upon seeing the materials I have devised, Carriacouans and other West Indians have reacted positively.

CONCLUSION

I suggest that the linguistic situation in places like Carriacou ought to be characterized as bilingual—or multilingual. I further suggest that in these contexts children should be first exposed to literacy in their native language, even if that language is a creolized variety of the official language. These suggestions are not made solely from the viewpoint of transitional bilingualism—that is, merely to help Creole speakers learn Export English. What is proposed here is a fundamental change away from traditional modes of education in the islands.

Such a change can be undertaken only after serious consideration and careful planning. But I believe that each human language enriches humanity as a whole by providing a different window through which to experience the universe. I think the native speakers of prestigious varieties of English can learn as much from Creole speakers as Creole speakers can learn from them.

NOTE

The fieldwork that provided the basis for this paper was supported by an Inter-American Foundation Master's Learning Fellowship on Social Change, which enabled me to spend April–August, 1979, in Carriacou. I also drew on my experience as a Peace Corps Volunteer in Carriacou 1971–1974. I wish to thank the good people of Carriacou and Grenada for taking me into their hearts and minds on both occasions.

APPENDIX

Carriacou Creole: Sample Orthography and Word List

CONSONANTS			VOWELS		
b	bobol[1]	swindle	a	gwana	iguana
ch	chups	teeth sucking	aa	faas	be forward
d	diil	work magic	e	fret	annoy, anger
f	fet	party	ei[2]	lavei	funeral wake
g	brangou	gossip	i	fig	banana
h	hosh	be quiet	ii	fiis	large meal
j	jombii	spirit	o	kom	come, go
k	kuku	cornmeal dish	ou[2]	koul	charcoal
l	lambii	conch meat	u	fut	leg, foot
m	maniku	opossum			
n	neks	another	ay	chayl	young person
ng	tong	town	ey	soley	bigeye fish
p	poupou	infant	oy	morokoy	tortoise
r	farin	cassava flour			
s	santopii	centipede	ā	sukuyā	vampire
sh	kyalabash	gourd	ē	tetshyē	tree boa
t	tatu	armadillo	ō	kōkosā	favor one of
v	veks	be angry			one's children
w	aawi	first plural			
y	aayu	second plural			
z	zutii	nettle			
zh	Monzhalu	Morne Jaloux			

[1] Stress is not phonemic at the word level and is not marked in these examples.

[2] *ei* and *ou* represent mid front and back vowels, not glides.

Part Three

Research and Evaluation

Extralinguistic Features in Bilingualism

BEN G. BLOUNT

Linguistic study of bilingualism has been focused on a number of well-developed topics, such as lexical borrowings, lexical shifts, linguistic interference, and interlanguage. One noteworthy topic in bilingualism, however, has not been well developed, despite its potential contributions to the field of study. This topic, extralinguistic features, is central to issues concerning the organization of discourse and the structure of social interaction among bilinguals. A case for the fundamental importance of extralinguistic features in the study of bilingualism is the goal of this paper.

In making the case, an account must be given of the importance of extralinguistic features in language research in general. That task in itself is not an easy one. (1) There are problems of definition and terminology. (2) Extralinguistic features play a dual role in language—a grammatical-referential one and an emotive-discourse one. (3) The entire subject has been relatively neglected in the study of language and communication. Yet the available evidence suggests that extralinguistic features carry a significant and even definitive load in communication. Given their importance in communication, and given the dual functional position that they occupy in verbal interaction, extralinguistic features appear especially relevant to the study of bilingualism. As a part of the code that has a significant communication function in each language, extralinguistic features are a potential source for misunderstanding in bilingual communication, although they are at the same time a potential source for increased creativity and richness in social interaction. These points will be elaborated below.

PROBLEMS OF DEFINITION AND MEASUREMENT

Organizationally, I should like to begin with a general definition of extralinguistic features and then proceed to an account of why, despite their importance, they have been relatively neglected in language research. That brief discussion will be followed by an account of the role of extralinguistic features in language structure, a review of their functions in discourse, and a summary of recent research in sociolinguistics that provides evidence for the importance of the features. Supportive evidence for the value of the features also will be presented from research on the language socialization of children.

Extralinguistic is used here to include the aspects of language that are generally referred to as intonation, prosody, and paralinguistics. Those aspects, more specifically defined, include stress and accent, pitch contours and intervals, rising and falling of pitch, fundamental frequency, intensity, duration and length, rhythmic structure, pause, breath groups, and secondary articulatory features such as labialization, nasalization, and palatalization. This definition is unusually broad, by design. The aim is to include all of the suprasegmental and paralinguistic dimensions of vocalization that can serve discourse functions. The specific dimensions that serve each of these functions are likely to differ to some degree across speech communities, and since the functions and differences cannot be predicted prior to empirical research, a broad definition seems advisable.

One additional matter concerning definitions should be stressed. The argument here is for a two-level approach to intonational, prosodic, and paralinguistic features, and the two levels can be referred to as linguistic and extralinguistic. The claim, for the sake of clarity, is that intonation, prosody, and paralinguistics can operate at both the grammatical and conversational levels. An intonational contour, for example, can mark an utterance as a question (a linguistic function), but the contour also may imply, in the context of the interaction, disbelief of a previous utterance (an extralinguistic function). It is not necessary, however, that all features be linguistic and extralinguistic at the same time. Vowel lengthening in English can indicate emphasis, but does not have any grammatical function. A feature, in other words, can be linguistic, extralinguistic, or both in function. The primary focus of the paper is on the second level, the extralinguistic, but that is a matter of emphasis not exclusion.

Although the importance of intonation, prosody, and paralinguistics in language description has been acknowledged for several decades, the tendency has been to relegate them to a peripheral position in linguistics. Linguists have concentrated their descriptive and analytic efforts on the segmental structure of language, often to the exclusion of suprasegmental ones. Several reasons can be ascertained, one of which is the difficulty of establishing and defining the units of analysis. There is a notable lack of standardization. Traditional orthography in linguistics reflects the difficulties; only a part of the intonational structure—to look solely at that aspect of language—is usually recorded, and linguists have differed considerably as to the appropriate procedures for recording tones. Intonation, to be certain, is difficult to study. Complex electronic instruments are necessary for accurate measurement and quantification, and results concerning amplitude, duration, and fundamental frequency are difficult to interpret. In the face of the problems of identity, classification, and measurement, linguists have generally tended to gloss over suprasegmental aspects of language.

A balanced view of extralinguistic factors in language description certainly must allow for a description of their relationship to segmentals. A range of views on the nature of the relationship is expressed in the literature. At one extreme, extralinguistic features can be seen as expressive of emotion but not as functionally significant aspects of language. At the other end of the spectrum, intonation has been viewed as the core structure of language, as a " . . . central, innately determined, and innately structured element of human language" (Lieberman 1980:187).

One of the more central and yet innovative perspectives on intonation and language structure has been provided by Dwight Bolinger. In a seminal paper entitled "Around the Edge of Language: Intonation," Bolinger (1964) addressed directly the question of how important intonation is in communication. At one level, he sees intonation as less central to communication than some other traits of language. "If it were [as central], we could not understand someone who speaks in a monotone; and, insofar as our comprehension of written language is due to its being a faithful reproduction of speech, we could not read" (1964:20). At another level, however, Bolinger addresses the question of importance by noting that the answer depends on knowing where the cost of misunderstanding becomes too high. His argument, in reconstruction, is as follows.

(1) Pitch is an important aspect of any language (as are tone, intonation, stress, and accent). (2) Languages utilize pitch in different
ways in their structure—for example, tone versus intonation languages. (3) The separation of emotion from other functions of pitch
modulations is extremely difficult—for example, "the rise and fall
of intonation can be thought of as grammatical signals of complete-
ness and incompleteness, or as emotive gauges of tension and relaxation" (Bolinger 1964:29). (4) The absence and especially the
misuse of pitch levels can lead to misunderstanding in either or both
senses—that is, emotional and/or grammatical. Difficulties in communication are especially likely to occur on the emotive side of the
features' duality, since societies certainly differ in terms of their
concepts of emotional displays and decorum.

The discussion here of the role of prosodic, intonational, and
paralinguistic features in language structure has been highly cursory
and intended only to establish a contrast with extralinguistic functions of the features. Two additional points are appropriate. First,
the relative neglect, the practical problems of study, and the frag-
mented approaches characterizing the subject render difficult any
historical assessment of accomplishments. One of the most distinguishing criteria of the subject is its resistance to standardization
and thus historical synthesis. The second point is that current research on prosody and intonation as properties of language addresses a wide variety of linguistic and extralinguistic functions. In
a recent state-of-the-art publication, subjects as far-ranging as bi-
narism and gradience, lexical functions, discourse structure, uni-
versals, innateness, ontogenesis, and even phylogenesis are discussed
(Waugh and van Schooneveld 1980). The scope of inquiry has certainly been enlarged in relation to earlier concerns, and includes
diverse linguistic, sociolinguistic, and biocultural elements. By extension, bilingualism can certainly be included in that list.

THE STUDY OF PROSODY, INTONATION, AND
PARALINGUISTICS IN SOCIOLINGUISTICS

The study of bilingualism encompasses, of course, a wide range
of phenomena: languages in contact, language and education, lan-

guage policy, and biculturalism, to name only some of the major topics in broad terms. What aspects or dimensions of bilingualism are the most relevant to the present discussion? Given that extra-linguistic features are functionally involved in communication, essentially any aspect of bilingual research would be relevant, germane, and certainly contributory. For practical purposes, however, we should ask which areas of research in bilingualism would benefit most directly from the study of prosody, intonation, and paralinguistics. The preliminary answer, at least, is sociolinguistics.

From its modern beginnings, approximately two decades ago, the major tenet of sociolinguistics has been that the language an individual speaks—that is, the choices that an individual makes in code selection—conveys social as well as referential and propositional meaning. The meaning of an utterance (a speech act) is constrained by the social conventions of a speech community and is predicted on the social attributions made in the context of the act and on the basis of patterned language usage. In those terms, a familiar topic in sociolinguistic studies, including bilingualism, has been code switching—that is, the social meanings attached to the alternative uses of different codes.

A fundamental question in code switching has been how codes are defined and identified. In some bilingual communities, the answer seems relatively clear-cut; the codes are languages—English, Spanish, French, or whatever. The issue of definition, however, is far more complex. Inspection of case studies reveals that numerous aspects of language have been identified as code, including the standard distinctions in language made on the bases of structure and function—dialects, lects, idiolects, registers, and styles. Among those aspects, phonological, lexical, and grammatical variants have been identified. In other words, virtually any aspect of language structure can be considered as code. Some aspects are more readily identifiable than others, such as distinct languages, but no aspect of language structures can be ruled out a priori. When attention is turned to prosody, intonation, and paralinguistics, one discovers, not surprisingly, that they are among the aspects that have proved elusive to analysis.

Not only are these features difficult to study as an aspect of code, for reasons discussed above, but an additional point must be considered. How something is said, as opposed to what is said, may determine meaning. As early as 1921, Edward Sapir recognized and wrote about the capacity of extralinguistic factors to override more strictly linguistic (that is, segmental and referential) factors in relation to meaning. Other linguists have subsequently noted that the referential function of an utterance can easily be altered by extralinguistic means. Examples are easy to create. Both "Bob loves Sue" and "Bob hates Sue" can mean exactly the opposite of the literal meaning, depending on how they are said.

Two recent attempts to describe the definitive communicative role that extralinguistic features can have are by Dell Hymes (1972; 1974). His efforts to identify, define, and classify components of speech events and ways of speaking led to the formulation of the concept of key. Key is viewed as a corollary to modality among grammatical categories, providing for the tone, manner, or spirit in which an act is done (Hymes 1974:57). Key is often signaled nonverbally, but, as Hymes notes, "it also commonly involves conventional units of speech too often disregarded in ordinary linguistic analysis, such as English aspiration and vowel length to signal emphasis" (1974:58). In other words, paralinguistic features—and, we can add, intonation and prosody—often signal the key in which a speech act or event is to be interpreted. The significance of key, again following Hymes (1974:58), is that it can override the meaning of the overt content of an act when it is in conflict with it.

Examples can easily be adduced to demonstrate the viability of the concept of key, to show that the meaning of a given unit of speech behavior can be mock or serious, painstaking or perfunctory, factual or fictive, depending on the signals given—verbal and/ or nonverbal—to the addressee or audience. Speakers can rely on their cultural knowledge to recognize the intended meaning. They can recognize, for example, that an exaggerated intonational contour can signal disbelief, as in

Jo^{hn} took the mon^{ey}

indicating that John could not possibly be a thief. The same utterance, however, made in light of common knowledge that John is a thief and that one would have been surprised if John had not taken the money, can signal feigned disbelief. In either case, the audience is given information as to how to interpret the speaker's meaning.

Unfortunately, relatively little information on the concept of key is available from naturalistic studies of conversation. Despite the obvious importance of key in communication, systematic sociolinguistic research is limited to a handful of studies.

One of these studies, by Gumperz and Herasimchuk (1972), was an analysis of verbal communication between teachers and students and among students in the first and second grades in Berkeley, California. The goal of their work was the elaboration of an empirical method of conversational analysis that would enable them to recover the social assumptions that underlie the interactional process (Gumperz and Herasimchuk 1972:99). Gumperz and Herasimchuk included prosodic and intonational information in their analysis of verbal interaction, operating under the theoretical assumption that the features were as important in interpreting the meaning of interactional exchanges as referential meaning or propositional content. The features were viewed as an optional set of communicative strategies that could be used alternatively with syntactic, lexical, or phonological variables, and the choice was viewed as a function of the speaker's background and his communicative intent (Gumperz and Herasimchuk 1972:114). Among the noteworthy findings of the study was the children's reliance on stress and intonation to mark their speech as showing confirmation, affirmation, question, challenge, following directions, emphasis, surprise, bluffing, and covering up errors (Gumperz and Herasimchuk 1972:114–115). The meaning of the interaction was, in effect, defined on the basis of the extralinguistic markings incorporated into the speech.

In another study, Gumperz (1978) noted that in everyday conversation, speakers shift constantly from one mode of speaking to another, from informal chats to serious discussion, from argument to humor. He asked the question of how shifts in perspective are signaled linguistically in conversational management. In a broader theoretical stance, Gumperz's concern was to show that linguistically marked strategies in conversational management are "culturally specific and that differential control of . . . strategies has important consequences for interpersonal and inter-ethnic relations, ethnic stereo-typing, and social mobility in modern urban societies"

(1978:4). In his analysis of conversational information among British English and Indian English speakers in London, Gumperz found that prosodic cues were highly subject to differential interpretation, with each group of native speakers missing, misconstruing, and in general misreading the cues that were vital to an understanding of the definition, or key, in which the speech was to be interpreted. To take only one example, a segment of speech by an Indian English speaker marked with weak stress for message emphasis was not perceived by a British English speaker, who consequently misunderstood the entire message that was intended.

The relevance of the Gumperz and Herasimchuk (1972) and Gumperz (1977) studies for bilingualism should be clear. Extralinguistic features, available to speakers as alternative markers of speech style, are definitive of intended meaning; and, to expand on that idea, they serve to key the framework in which the speech is to be interpreted. The ability of interactants to utilize these features efficiently and appropriately is a product of cultural knowledge. Any face-to-face interaction in bilingual situations is subject to the constraints that are posed by the culturally defined extralinguistic features. These features have to be identified and described empirically, and the normal expectation is that each speech community will have different systems. Bilinguals are subject to at least two sets of culturally defined features. The potential for misunderstanding messages is increased because of the dual system and their possible relationships, but the possibility for creative, enriched verbal exchange is also heightened because more expressive opportunities are available.

A rudimentary framework for ascertaining the significance of the extralinguistic features is now available, and, given the critical role that these features have in communication, increased knowledge about them should be a priority research endeavor. Since, again, the role of extralinguistic features in bilingual communication is essentially unexplored, virtually any research would add to the needed stock of knowledge on this important subject. As an illustration of the richness of intonational, prosodic, and paralinguistic features in speech, a brief report is given here on the utilization of those features in the language of socialization in English and Spanish.

A STUDY OF ENGLISH- AND SPANISH-SPEAKING PARENTS

In a research project begun in 1972 in Austin, Texas, the speech of English- and Spanish-speaking parents to young children was tape-recorded and analyzed to discover properties of the speech that made it (1) recognizable to native speakers as a speech register suitable for addressing infants and young children, and (2) suitable for eliciting and sustaining the interaction of the children. Previous research had identified a small number of special speech features, including exaggerated intonation and paralinguistic features such as labialization (Ferguson 1964). In the Austin study, twenty-three prosodic and paralinguistic features were identified (Blount and Padgug 1977), and that number is certainly not exhaustive.

Speech addressed to infants and young children who are only beginning to acquire a rudimentary verbal capacity is highly marked with the special, or extralinguistic, features. Almost all of the parental utterances to the nine children in the study contained at least one feature—more than 97 percent were marked—and the number of features per parental utterance was high: 239.6 per hundred utterances in English and 242.2 per hundred utterances in Spanish. Because of the extra work it must perform in attracting an infant's attention, directing the attention to an activity, and sustaining the attention throughout the activity, parental speech probably represents the most extreme speech register in all societies in terms of the abundant utilization of extralinguistic features. An interesting note, however, is that the social meaning of an episode of parent/ child interaction is defined by the extralinguistic features—that is, in terms of attention management—in essentially the same way that episodes of interaction among adult speakers of a language can be keyed in regard to meaning (see Blount and Kempton 1976; Blount 1981). The onset of interaction, the regulation of turn-taking (conversational) behavior, and the relationship of the joint parent/child behavior to the environment are regulated by extralinguistic features. Extralinguistic features have similar roles in structuring social interaction among parents and infants as in adult discourse. In parental speech, the dosage of features is likely to be more profuse.

Because of the differential utilization of extralinguistic features in their speech, some comparisons of English-speaking and Spanish-speaking parents are instructive. Table 1 shows the ten most frequently occurring extralinguistic features in the speech of the English-speaking parents collectively and of the Spanish-speaking parents collectively. The speech across recording sessions (approximately twelve sessions with each of the nine children, each session roughly thirty minutes) is treated compositely. The figures represent rate measures—that is, the number of times per hundred utterances that a feature was used in parental speech.

As inspection of Table 1 shows that English and Spanish parental speech registers show considerable similarity. Seven of the ten most frequently occurring extralinguistic features are found in each language, and parents in each language group use Exaggerated intonation more frequently than any other feature. The rates for High pitch, Lowered volume, Lengthened vowel, and Falsetto are very similar. There are, however, clear differences in parental selection of features across languages. English-speaking parents use (1) Exaggerated intonation 22 percent more than do Spanish-speaking parents; (2) Breathiness approximately two and a half times as much as the Spanish-speaking parents; and (3) Creaky voice, Tenseness, and Low pitch considerably more than do the Spanish-speaking

Table 1. Composite Rate Measures and Relative Ranking for Each Extralinguistic Speech Feature, English and Spanish

ENGLISH		SPANISH	
Feature	Rate	Feature	Rate
1. Exaggerated intonation	67.2	1. Exaggerated intonation	52.4
2. Breathiness	29.1	2. High pitch	31.2
3. High pitch	25.4	3. Stress	25.8
4. Lowered volume	22.9	4. Lowered volume	22.7
5. Lengthened vowel	22.5	5. Raised volume	22.6
6. Creaky voice	14.4	6. Lengthened vowel	20.5
7. Stress	11.2	7. Fast tempo	19.6
8. Tenseness	11.0	8. Slow tempo	18.3
9. Falsetto	8.5	9. Breathiness	12.2
10. Low pitch	7.0	10. Falsetto	11.0

parents. In turn, the Spanish-speaking parents use: (1) Stress approximately twice as often; and (2) Raised volume, Fast tempo, and Slow tempo considerably more than do English-speaking parents. To summarize the differences: the English-speaking parents use comparatively more breath control, tenseness, and pitch modulation, whereas Spanish-speaking parents use relatively more stress, volume control, and rate/tempo variation. To refine these dimensions even further: English-speaking parents tend to use more voice control on a lax/tense dimension (intensity), while Spanish parents tend to rely more on volume prominence and fastness/slowness (rhythm) of speech. Although these results are on the basis of composites, and variations among individuals should be considered, they suggest a considerably different approach in parental speech registers in English and Spanish. To the extent that the extralinguistic features key social meaning, and these meanings are acquired developmentally through interaction, they are likely to be important dimensions of meaning in the adult system, including the systems of bilinguals in English and Spanish.

CONCLUSIONS

The dual nature of prosodic, intonational, and paralinguistic features in the organization of meaning makes them excellent topics for linguistic and sociolinguistic research. A study of their linguistic properties addresses important questions about their grammatical functions, whereas a focus on their extralinguistic properties provides an avenue for investigating the structure of social interaction. As extralinguistic features, prosody, intonation, and paralinguistics provide acoustic signals that members of a speech community utilize to organize their verbal interactions. The features are used to mark and thus key discourse so as to provide interactants with the signals that allow them to select meaning appropriate to the speech situation. The features, in other words, provide a means whereby speakers can produce markers of intent in their verbalizations, and the features, as markers, give a structure to the flow of conversation.

Fluent bilinguals have by definition two culturally defined sets of extralinguistic features. Given the definitive role that the features can have in the organization of discourse, their description in bilingualism appears to have special significance. The task of unraveling the complexities of code choice and social consequence in bilingualism would be facilitated by a greater stock of knowledge about the central role that prosody, intonation, and paralinguistics play in the cultural organization of meaning.

NOTE

Helpful comments and editorial assistance have been provided by Dr. Carolyn Ehardt. Any shortcomings of the paper remain, however, mine.

Researching Bilingualism in the Classroom

Andrew D. Cohen

As bilingual education continues to be a prominent force on the North American educational scene, evaluation of bilingual programs is becoming increasingly refined. Practicing and prospective evaluators are now able to obtain extensive if not exhaustive descriptions of what it is they may or should evaluate (see, for example, Bissell 1979; Burry 1979).

Program evaluators are often brought in from outside to increase the objectivity of the evaluation, and they are often requested to focus on summative evaluation. If the evaluators are external to the program, they may, consequently, have limited knowledge about the range of special factors pertaining to the particular bilingual program. Hence, it seems reasonable for teachers to think more about steps that they can take to ensure accurate evaluation of their programs. The teacher can play an invaluable role both in guiding evaluators in the design of evaluation by identifying key variables to consider and in helping to interpret the results once the data have been analyzed.

It may be argued that it is not a teacher's business to get involved in evaluation. It was found in one study (Cohen and Roll 1979), for example, that teachers had difficulties adhering to stringent guidelines for collecting oral ("natural") data from children in their classrooms, for transcribing these data, and for scoring them. On the other hand, teachers' assistance in designing evaluation and in interpreting results may be crucial if meaningful evaluation is to take place. Teachers can assist in evaluation by describing what they already are aware of and by turning their awareness and powers of observation to classroom phenomena they did not previously attend.

Without some assistance from project staff—and teachers seem to be the best source—evaluators may draw inappropriate conclusions about the nature of bilingual education classrooms, conclusions that lead to statements that misrepresent the reality of these classrooms. A recent large-scale evaluation of bilingual schooling (American Institutes for Research 1977), for example, came under criticism for failing to pay adequate attention to factors characterizing the actual bilingual education classroom, such as distinguishing student and program characteristics.

What are the advantages of accurate evaluation? Why should the teacher be motivated to participate in evaluation efforts, however minimally? A recent convocation of experts (Bissell 1979) produced the following list of potential benefits of evaluation reports.

1. Identifying project components that are highly successful.
2. Describing a project to parents of participants and nonparticipants to encourage interest in it.
3. Informing decision makers about the rationale for, and the benefits of, the project.
4. Conveying information about the project to other locations and institutions of higher education.
5. Providing a morale booster for teachers and administrative staff, who see the evaluation report as testimony to their efforts in making the project work.

Obviously, there is also the real possibility that evaluation will point up certain weaknesses, and the concerned teacher should welcome such information along with the suggested modifications that might stem from such findings.

We will focus our attention on some of the principles of classroom description—principles that are intended to be particularly relevant to evaluation of classroom aspects of bilingual education programs. The principles selected for discussion are as follows: (1) program model, type, and design; (2) student characteristics; (3) instructional methods; (4) teacher and student language-use patterns; (5) functional language ability; and (6) development of language skills.

PRINCIPLE 1: PROGRAM MODEL, TYPE, AND DESIGN

Since the particular program model, type, and design of bilingual schooling can have an important effect on evaluation results, the individual aspects should be carefully identified and described. The program model refers to the basic broad classes of bilingual programs—for example, transitional, maintenance, enrichment, restorative. The program type refers to the specific characteristics of the particular model—for example, a maintenance program that promotes minority language maintenance in all subject areas versus one that focuses on maintenance in selected areas. The program design refers to characteristics of the particular program type—for example, within a full bilingual maintenance program, the first and second languages are both introduced in early stages and emphasized equally later on. (See Trueba 1979 for a complete discussion of the distinctions between model, type, and design.)

Regarding the program model, the evaluator would need to examine and indicate the following in the report: *Is the program transitional, maintenance, enrichment, or restorative?*

Regarding the program type: *How is bilingual instruction actually implemented? Are the two languages used concurrently as media of instruction? Are they used alternately—for example, mornings in one language and afternoons in the other; Mondays in one language and Tuesdays in another? Is special instruction in English as a second language provided?*

How much of the day—in actual classroom minutes or hours—is reserved for bilingual schooling?

Is the program team-taught with two or more teachers? Are there one or more paid aides in the classroom?

Regarding the program design: *What are the ethnic and language backgrounds of the students? How are the students grouped in the classroom—for example, homogeneously or heterogeneously by native language?*

Are the students in a self-contained classroom for bilingual instruction or do they receive bilingual instruction in several classrooms—as through team-teaching, departmentalized instruction, or pullout programs?

*How many of the school's classrooms and which grade levels
have bilingual instruction? How many schools in the district are
included in the bilingual program?*

Across model, type, and design: *Have there been major changes
in any of the above-mentioned factors over time—that is, is the
program stable or changing?*

PRINCIPLE 2: STUDENT CHARACTERISTICS

Accurate characterization of students is not easy, but it is essential if the results of evaluation are to be meaningful. Current theories about bilingualism and cognitive development have helped
provide more precise ways of describing student characteristics than
in the past. For example, the following variables should be considered:

1. The student's absolute proficiency in academic and nonacademic
contexts for each of two languages, not just relative proficiency
(usually referred to as language dominance). In other words, what
seems to be the student's total grasp of vocabulary in both languages?
What is the student's control of the grammar of both languages? For
example, the student may appear to have control of most, if not all, of
the grammatical structures in both languages that a native speaker
the same age would have. The concept of absolute proficiency is an
important one. Sometimes statements of relative proficiency are
misleading because they do not indicate limitations that students may
have in certain areas—such as vocabulary—of both languages.

2. The student's level of cognitive/academic language proficiency
in the classroom. A theory now has been proposed that bilingual
children need to develop proficiency in at least one of their languages
above a basic threshold level in order to develop the cognitive skills
related to literacy and to other verbal/academic tasks (Cummins 1978).
Teachers may have some insights into the ease or difficulty with
which particular students learn new concepts in class. They may be
aware of particular students who have trouble learning a mathematical
concept when presented both in English and in the minority language.
The reason for the conceptual difficulty may be that the students
have difficulty conceptualizing altogether. They need to develop their
cognitive/academic language proficiency more fully (according to
the theory), perhaps with an initial emphasis on the mother tongue—
the minority language. This cognitive/academic language proficiency is

to be distinguished from what Cummins (1980) calls "basic interpersonal communicative skills"—that is, the oral fluency skills necessary to function in everyday interpersonal contexts. The teacher is in a good position to determine whether the student has this basic communicative proficiency but not the cognitive and academic language proficiency necessary for success at school.

In considering student characteristics, we would also want to include more traditional variables such as the following.

3. Identification of the student's ethnic group, number of years in the United States, language use outside school, and socioeconomic status.

4. The student's educational history, particularly the years the child has been in the bilingual program. For example, one student may have attended an English-only kindergarten and entered the bilingual program in grade one; another student may have been enrolled in a monolingual first-language program in the native country for three years before coming to the United States and entered the bilingual program in grade three.

PRINCIPLE 3: INSTRUCTIONAL METHODS

As teachers know only too well from daily experience in the classroom, the instructional method in a bilingual program is not simply bilingual education, although it makes evaluation easier to look at it that way. In reality, the success of a program may well depend on the nature of the specific approach to oral skills, to reading, and to subject matter. With respect to an oral language program, for example, the evaluator needs to know the following.

1. *Is there formal oral language instruction in the second language? If so, to what extent do the instructional methods emphasize meaningful communication as opposed to focusing strictly on form?* For example, memory of dialogs and pattern practice drills may emphasize form extensively and perhaps exclusively, whereas practicing utterances in meaningful contexts and engaging in communicative exercises may emphasize natural language more.

2. *Are there teacher guidelines for the program?* For example, in some programs teachers use ready-made lesson plans prepared commercially or by the local district. Such lesson plans take the form of actual scripts that the teachers are to read. If there are guidelines, it is useful to know how carefully teachers adhere to them.

With respect to reading, the evaluator needs to know the following.

1. *In which language did the students begin reading? Their native language? The second language? Or did they start reading in both languages simultaneously?*

2. *Is there a particular reading method or combination of methods being used for teaching reading in each language—for example, the phonemic approach, the linguistic-phonemic approach, the language-experience approach?* (See Aukerman 1971; Weaver 1980.)

3. *Are the materials for teaching reading in both languages equally good?* Sometimes materials in one language (usually English) have been field-tested more extensively, and only the most interesting and challenging stories and exercises have been retained in the final commercial version. Field testing also helps to establish whether the particular approach to reading seems best for the majority of students in the given language. Sometimes one reading series includes a better system for giving students feedback about their progress— either through step-by-step programmed activities or through meaningful tests at the end of each unit. Some materials are better than others at recycling previous material to reinforce vocabulary and structures presented in the earlier material.

4. *Assuming all students are using the same method, is the material sequenced the same for all of them?*

5. *Do students who are using the same readers progress at the same pace or at different paces? Do they progress by group or individually, as through the contract approach, whereby each student makes a contract with the teacher as to how much he or she will read?*

6. *Are students grouped by ability, by interest, or homogeneously according to language dominance? Is there total-class instruction?*

7. *Is scheduling flexible? Are students in nongraded classrooms?*

8. *What is the ratio of teachers and paraprofessionals to children? What is the language proficiency of the instructors in each of their languages?*

9. *What efforts have been made in the classroom to promote biliteracy—for example, bulletin boards, store corners, reading centers, signs, school/classroom post office, newspapers, magazines, books?*

PRINCIPLE 4: TEACHER AND STUDENT LANGUAGE-USE PATTERNS

The teacher's choice of language for classroom management, for discussing content, and for chatting with colleagues during breaks may well transmit to the students attitudes about the two languages. The teacher's language use may, for example, mark one language—usually the minority language—as less acceptable or perhaps even inferior. It is for this reason that it is advisable to audiotape or even videotape language-use patterns. Such external, objective measures help teachers base their self-assessments upon actual behavior rather than personal impressions.

The evaluator needs to know whether the teacher uses one language only for various portions of the day or if a particular teacher uses only one language. If, for example, the teacher moves back and forth between languages, is this switching patterned and purposeful, as in the concurrent approach (see Jacobson 1979), or unsystematic? Switching from one language to another—even carefully planned switching—may promote interference between the two languages (Cohen 1975, Ch. 8), particularly interference from English when speaking the minority language, since the minority language is usually the more susceptible to erosion in a society where another language is dominant. In other words, this type of erosion of the native language, or "backlash interference," as Jakobovits (1970) has called it, takes place in the Spanish of native Spanish speakers living in an English-speaking country, in the English of English speakers living in a Hebrew-speaking country, and so forth.

To understand language-use patterns in the classroom, it is important to describe not only the language-use patterns of the teacher but also the language-use patterns of the students. Student language-use patterns may not conform to those of the teacher, although they are often prompted by the teacher's patterns. The language that students use for negotiating or managing activities among themselves, for responding to the teacher, and for thinking to themselves while reading or while trying to solve problems may be somewhat conditioned by the teacher's language-use behavior. However, students' language-use patterns may also conform to their own patterns of social interaction in the classroom.

If the program is two-way, in that monolingual English speakers are learning through the minority language while minority-language speakers are learning through English, the evaluator may wish to know whether there is genuine two-way bilingual language use, or whether English-language use prevails among the monolingual English speakers. Monolingual English-speaking minority students may be particularly resistant to using the minority language. It may be that the monolingual English speakers consciously or unconsciously sensed negative attitudes in the community at large toward the minority language and felt it better to focus on the majority-group language. Perhaps their older siblings or parents had already made that attitudinal decision before they were born and transmitted it to them. There also may be other reasons for English-speaking minority students to resist using the minority language.

PRINCIPLE 5: FUNCTIONAL LANGUAGE ABILITY

Language researchers are realizing that there is more to achieving language proficiency than mastering grammatical inflections, prepositions, negation, and interrogative forms. Assessment of speaking skills in bilingual programs has traditionally consisted of a tally of such errors (see Cohen 1975, Ch. 8; Cohen in press). Thus the focus has been largely on deviance or on what the student does not seem to have mastered. A complementary and perhaps more productive approach is to assess what the student can do with the language, particularly the ability to function successfully in it. In this functional approach, the emphasis is on the student's command of communicative functions—that is, the ability to perform certain speech acts in the classroom, to comprehend what they mean when others perform them, and to comprehend their meaning when they occur in reading texts. A speech act is the act of doing something in saying something. For example, native-speaking children know that they have a variety of ways to request something. So, in order to request that someone open a window, they may say, "It's hot in here." This declarative statement would then serve as a request (the speech act).

The following is a tentative list of those speech acts identified by one researcher as most crucial to communication in the elementary school classroom environment: pleas, suggestions, requests, demands, orders, warnings, threats, promises, authorizations, and apologies (Walters 1980). As it turns out, the speaker rarely uses the direct form of the speech act (for example, "I request the eraser"), but, rather, uses other strategies such as asking about ability ("Could you pass the eraser?"), asking about location ("Where's the eraser?"), expressing a need ("I need the eraser").

PRINCIPLE 6: DEVELOPMENT OF LANGUAGE SKILLS

The way that each of a student's two languages develops in a bilingual program may be of interest, particularly in cases where the student is having difficulties. Development here refers to the incremental changes that may occur over time in each of a student's language skills: speaking, listening, reading, and writing. Such information is not necessarily recoverable from evaluation of interim and end-of-year achievement in a program. Teachers can provide some information, however anecdotal—for example, a description of problems that the student who is not very proficient in the native language has when learning through both languages simultaneously. The skill that has received extensive attention—perhaps because we seem to know the most about how to teach it—is reading. Perhaps teachers could write down comments that the students make or have the students explain the reading strategies that they are using to get meaning from the passage (see Hosenfeld 1979).

Even if evaluations include measures of achievement more frequently than once a year, a certain amount of information is lost in the testing process because evaluators do not know what process students use to answer test questions. I am suggesting here that the teacher can use the evaluator's standardized reading test—and tests of other skills as well—as a vehicle for better understanding where the student experiences difficulty in reading. Perhaps the teachers could go over certain items on a test with the students, discussing how the students read the stimulus material and their reasoning behind choosing certain answers (see Cohen 1980b, Ch. 3). It may be that a student answers certain test items wrong because of limited reading ability. A discussion session with the student could help pinpoint the source of the difficulty, if the teacher does not know it already—for example, problems decoding letters, limited vocabulary.

It is also possible that the processes whereby the student arrives at answers to certain reading items are well based—that is, based on sound reasoning, strong powers of inference, and so forth. But the items themselves may have certain confusing properties. Of course, the main purpose of such an exercise is not to critique the particular reading test but, rather, to determine what specific problems the poor reader is having in trying to read—and specifically when trying to read material contained in reading tests. By talking with students about their answering strategies, it is possible to obtain some of this information.

OTHER AREAS OF CONCERN FOR EVALUATION

The presentation of the six principles was purposely slanted toward evaluation of language-related, classroom-centered issues in bilingual education. The main question that prompted the identification of such principles was "What makes bilingual education evaluation different from other kinds of school evaluation?" And the answer seemed to be "The use of two languages as vehicles for instruction." Thus, it is no coincidence that all of the principles deal in some way with language-related evaluation. This is not to say that evaluation of mathematics, social studies, science, and so forth is of less importance, but simply that evaluation in these areas has a more solid base of experience to draw from, whereas bilingual education evaluation is a relatively recent phenomenon. Only in the past several years has the field of bilingual evaluation been able to boast an array of assessment instruments. (See, for example, Dissemination Center for Bilingual Bicultural Education 1975; Silverman et al. 1976; Pletcher, Noa, and Russell 1978.)

The newest aspect of evaluation in the subject areas may in fact be that subject-matter tests now have to (or should) appear in at least two languages. But here again, the problem is primarily one of language. Is the minority-language test a translation from the English version? If so, is it a meaningful translation, given the sociocultural context of the target-language group? If the test is not a translation and was not meant to be, then are the English- and minority-language tests comparable in scope and difficulty? There are many other questions that could also be posed.

There are areas of concern for evaluation of bilingual education programs that are not taken up in the six principles discussed previously. One concern is that of setting the school in its context. Mention of context was made only in passing, with regard to Principle 1, the program model, type, and design. Various aspects of school context could be described and evaluated, such as the ethnic composition of the school staff, the locus of the program within the school structure, the degree of institutionalization of the program, and the extent of the program's dependency upon federal funds as opposed to local funding sources. The classroom teacher may have some insights to share with the evaluator in these areas. The evaluator is likely to obtain some of this information from school administrators, including the director of the bilingual program, if there is one.

Another concern is the cultural background of the students, given their particular ethnic affiliations. The role of culture in bilingual education is a broad matter, and has been treated in detail elsewhere (see, for example, Saville-Troike 1978). Suffice it to say here that an evaluator might be concerned with how the student's cultural background influences the behavior that is being assessed. For example, when assessing language-use patterns, the evaluator should probably want to be cognizant of any cultural factors that would influence both whom students talk to, in what context, what they talk about, and which language or language variety they use. It may be misleading, in other words, to use some majority-group framework for judging conversational skills and appropriate choice of language, when the minority culture would have another framework. For example, acceptable ways of requesting things in the minority language may appear rude in mainstream conversation.

Take the example of a simple request to a student to open the door. In the minority language, it may be perfectly polite to give the direct command, "Open the door." Depending on the circumstances, such a command may sound too rude in English. It may be necessary to mitigate the request through a question such as, "Could you open the door for me?" Also, what appears to be a surprisingly high use of English by minority-language students in a bilingual program may result from the students' desire to please the teacher by using the teacher's native language, which in this case is English. And if the teacher is a native speaker of the minority language, the student may likewise use the minority language more. Such student accommodation of the teacher's native language has actually been seen to take place (see, for example, Bruck, Shultz, and Rodríguez-Brown 1979).

Culture also proves to be a crucial element in any formal testing situation. As Saville-Troike (1978:49) points out: "Testing is itself a social event. . . . Evaluation instruments can never be considered culturally neutral, no matter how 'objective' their format." We could, for example, ask whether the attitudinal measure referred to under Principle 1 is perhaps more culturally specific to the Anglo culture in the United States. For example, is it culturally specific to conceptualize attitudes in terms of scales such as "self-acceptance"? Or even if such scales might have validity in other cultures, would the scales be composed of similar items, worded in similar ways? For example, in another culture, perhaps self-acceptance is not so innerdirected a concept as in the United States. In another culture, accepting oneself may refer first and foremost to being a loyal member of the community. Thus, an item assessing self-acceptance in that culture might investigate the student's sense of commitment to the community. The item would also most likely be phrased in language consistent with the culture, in this case, in terms of commitment to the community.

Also, there is more to be said about the academic characteristics of the students being evaluated. The emphasis in the discussion of Principle 2, student characteristics, is on language and on the relationship between language and cognition. The students' ethnicity and the history of their involvement in bilingual schooling are also touched on. However, much more than this goes into a student's academic profile.

How well has the student performed in the content areas until now? How well is the student performing at this point? For instance, the student may have completed two years of schooling in some other country and may have been weak in mathematics there. Or the student may have been in a bilingual program from the start and may have had difficulties grasping science concepts, even when they were presented exclusively in the student's native tongue. It may be that the difficulties are due largely to the nature of the instruction.

For example, the student and the teacher or teachers may not have got along well together, the curriculum materials may not have motivated the student adequately, or the way the two languages were used in the classroom may not have been appropriate. In the past, some educators felt that bilingual children's difficulties in school were most likely a result of limited intellectual ability. Work over the past decade has shown that such assumptions were ill-founded. For example, DeAvila developed a Piagetian-based measure of cognitive development consisting of five subscales for each of two levels (K-3, grades 4–6) (DeAvila and Havassy 1974; DeAvila and Duncan 1978). He then tested it with more than six thousand Mexican American children, and found their cognitive performance to be similar to that of Anglos. He found differences, however, in school-related achievement. He concluded that these differences were due to linguistic and sociocultural biases inherent in most of the currently used educational approaches (DeAvila and Duncan 1979).

Another factor that was only partially touched on is that of teacher variables. With respect to Principle 4, teacher and student language-use patterns, it is suggested that teachers may consciously or unconsciously mark the minority language as less prestigious. There are, of course, a number of other teacher factors, such as teacher personality, the extent and nature of teacher training, the teacher's proficiency in the two languages, the teacher's experience teaching through the two languages, the teacher's ability to provide a learning challenge that is compatible with the learning potential of the individual student, and the teacher's ability to lead discussions in class so as to encourage student learning. A comprehensive listing of teacher factors relating specifically to bilingual instruction has appeared elsewhere (Center for Applied Lingusitics 1974), as well as extensive suggestions for teacher-preparation programs in bilingual education at the undergraduate and graduate levels (Acosta and Blanco 1978).

There is the problem, however, that teacher variables are not easy to evaluate objectively under any circumstances. A language-use variable, such as the teacher's choice of language for a particular activity or moment within an activity, may be easier to assess than variables concerning how effective the teacher's system of discipline is or how affirmatively the teacher responds to students' attempts to express themselves. Even if such teacher variables are assessed effectively, books like those by Dunkin and Biddle (1974) and Brophy and Good (1974) seem to have dispelled the notion that teaching patterns such as limited "teacher talk" (Flanders 1970) will produce more beneficial results than extensive teacher talk. Although a theoretical model might suggest that teachers should not talk too much, Dunkin and Biddle (1974) concluded from a review of various studies that there was no relationship between the extent of teacher talk and student achievement or attitudes. The study also found, among other things, that accepting students' ideas, praising students, and asking frequent questions did not necessarily lead to greater achievement on the part of the students.

Even if we could somehow accurately describe a number of characteristics of a particular teacher or teachers in a bilingual program, how could we ensure that teachers in a control or comparison group (if there is one) display similar characteristics for comparison purposes? We usually cannot. Hence, we have the phenomenon, as found in the Redwood City study, of comparison-group teachers having many more years of experience in teaching English reading than bilingual-program teachers (Cohen 1975). Tucker and Cziko (1978) suggest that the best that one can do is to make sure that experimental- and control-class teachers are equally qualified. For this, we could turn to the list of qualifications for bilingual-teacher certification developed by the Center for Applied Linguistics (1974).

The six principles also do not speak to the issue of parent and community involvement in the program. Actually, there is growing concern regarding the roles of parents and of the community at large in the working of a bilingual program. For example, are parents simply a group to be placated or informed, or are they a body that is to impose checks and balances, or even help to introduce change (Rodríguez 1979)? And at what stages of program development (planning, implementation, or evaluation) are parents to be involved (Cruz 1979)?

Although time-consuming to document, characteristics of the local community can provide the evaluator invaluable information to aid in interpreting results. In reality, very little research has been conducted regarding, for example, bilingual-language proficiency and language-use patterns of parents in the community, parental support for bilingual schooling, or parental knowledge about bilingual programs (Cohen 1979). Knowledge about the language-proficiency and language-use patterns of parents of children in bilingual programs can contribute to the construction and selection of bilingual curriculum materials appropriate to the language background of the students. Such knowledge could, for example, help avert the development of materials that are too demanding in one language and not demanding enough in the other. Longitudinal research on language-use patterns of families with children in bilingual programs can help inform program administrators about whether program language goals are being met (for example, whether the minority language is being maintained, if this is a goal; see Cohen 1975, Ch. 9). Sometimes information about the local community can be gleaned from school visits with parents, from home visits, from school trips, and in other ways.

Regarding parental involvement in the bilingual program, it is not a given that parents of children in a bilingual program are supportive of the program. Yet initial misgivings about bilingual schooling may give way to more positive feelings as parents see the results of the program. If parents are to make genuine choices about the bilingual schooling of their children, then they may need to be involved in program specifics at the three levels of planning, implementation, and evaluation, rather than simply to endorse an abstraction, namely bilingual education. It is possible that teachers can help parents play this sort of role and can help evaluators understand what the parental and community roles actually are in a given case as well as what they could be.

There is still a need to improve questioning procedures in order to tap parental knowledge and opinions about bilingual schooling. Perhaps teachers can help obtain information beyond pat answers to interview questions. What is needed is an informal, natural environment in which honest comments would emerge. Sometimes evaluators can effect this, and sometimes they cannot. Teachers may be able to help.

CONCLUSIONS

This paper has concentrated on how teachers can assist evalua-tors, because clearly the teachers themselves do not have much time in their schedules for conducting evaluation, particularly formally. But teachers may have time for more informal evaluation. In fact, some of the descriptive information about the classroom may be relatively inaccessible to anyone but the teacher, since it reflects cumulative insights gleaned from repeated encounters with students on a daily basis.

Let us take a look now, in summary, at some of the activities that have been suggested for teachers: (1) gather descriptive facts about how the bilingual schooling model, type, and design actually func-tion on a daily basis; (2) provide data on students' language profi-ciency and on their cognitive functioning—that is, their grasp of concepts—both in their native language and in their second lan-guage; (3) describe the teaching methods in the program (the ap-proaches that are used on a daily basis), the teaching materials and how they are used, and any changes that occur in methods and materials over time; (4) gather data, possibly tape-recorded, on teacher and student language-use patterns; (5) report on student fa-cility with speech acts (like requesting, suggesting, and apologiz-ing) in both languages; (6) pay special attention to reading development in both languages, particularly among students with reading difficulties, so that the teacher can provide insights to eval-uators about what the reading test results mean in these cases.

It is a tall order to ask teachers to add more activities to their already busy schedules, but it may just be that activities such as those listed here will be welcome additions—assuming teachers are not already engaged in such activities, which they well may be. Not only would teachers increase the information for evaluators about what is being evaluated but, at the same time, they might also bring their own conceptions of the program into sharper focus.

Federal Research Directions
in Bilingual Education

CHARLOTTE I. MILLER AND RENÉ F. CÁRDENAS

This work is the result of the collaboration of an applied anthropologist (Miller) and a project evaluator (Cárdenas) in interpreting their understanding and experience in the area of federal bilingual education evaluation research for a wider audience of anthropologists. In this paper we discuss the issue of federal bilingual education programs in the United States and research being carried out to evaluate and improve their effectiveness. We first discuss sources of bilingual education funding. Then we look at evaluation research specifically as it applies to bilingual education. From there, we review the federal orientation toward bilingual education evaluation research methods and the contracting procedures that determine them, describing under what conditions such research is undertaken and by whom. Finally, we illustrate some of the points we have made with a list of research projects and more detailed case study of Development Associates' current project for which Cárdenas is principal investigator.

We want to make it clear at the outset that we do not officially represent the views of the federal agencies discussed, nor are we taking a particular position in favor of, or against, a particular policy in the area of bilingual education. We are reporting on our perceptions and analysis of the process of bilingual education evaluation research and the federal directions in future funding for such research.

BILINGUAL EDUCATION:
DEFINITIONS, MANDATE, AND FUNDING

Cultural anthropologists and linguists, as illustrated by the present collection of papers, have much to say on the subject of bilingualism and its impact on education—and vice versa. The social science definitions of bilingualism and education are not necessarily the same as those used by most Americans when speaking of bilingual education. In the United States, the term has come to refer to particular government-sponsored programs for children with "limited English proficiency," often referred to by the acronym LEP. In other words, it does not refer to French classes for native speakers of English or Berlitz courses for consultants traveling abroad. Bilingual education, in short, has become identified as a program for immigrants and non-English-speaking natives of the United States, clearly marginal to the political power centers. Bilingual education is advocated by groups that see the value of maintenance of language use and cultural practices other than those associated with English-language use. Owing to differences of priorities, advocates and detractors of bilingual education programs have become polarized. Detractors include assimilationist immigrants and taxpayers who resent paying for a program from which they do not directly benefit.

Nevertheless, bilingual education of some type has been mandated by statutory law as well as court decree. In 1974, the Supreme Court ruled that schools could not deny children an education because of a language barrier (*Lau* v. *Nichols*). Thus, some steps taken by the government to provide equal opportunities to LEP children have been known as "Lau remedies." Since that ruling, four hundred school districts have negotiated compliance agreements through the Office of Civil Rights in the Education Department (*Educational Daily*, Aug. 15, 1980).

Two major agency sources for funding of programs and projects in bilingual education (including Lau remedies) are the Office of Bilingual Education and Minority Language Affairs (OBEMLA), and the Office of Program Management of the Department of Education (which does evaluation research). Other federal programs or activities that assist or contribute to bilingual education include: (1) The Emergency School Aid Act (ESAA), which makes available bilingual grants to school districts for carrying out desegregation programs involving children who require bilingual education. (2) Title IV of the Civil Rights Act of 1964, which provides funds for hiring advisory specialists in bilingual education and for staff training. (3) The Follow Through Program, whose funds benefit bilingual instruction in that the program provides assistance to children in kindergarten through third grade who were previously enrolled in Head Start or similar programs, some of which have bilingual components. (4) The Right-to-Read Program (Title I impact), which provides funds to over one hundred preelementary and elementary projects throughout the country, including many bilingual projects. (5) The Office of Indian Education, which has provided discretionary grants for projects that focus on the needs of the limited-English-proficient American Indian population. (6) The Teacher Corps Program of the Department of Education, which sponsors some bilingual projects. (7) The Administration for Children, Youth, and Family, which has had projects that trained Head Start workers to teach in bilingual/bicultural situations.

Programs are actually administered by state and local governments through their agencies. Many local programs receive funding from several sources at once. This paper, however, deals only with aspects of the OBEMLA programs and the Office of Program Management's evaluations of those programs.

The evaluation of OBEMLA programs have been authorized by the Elementary and Secondary Education Act (ESEA) Title VII in the Education Amendments of 1978. These amendments called for an ambitious program of evaluation research in response to congressional mandates for information on the beneficiaries and programs of bilingual education: identifying the children who need it; determining how may it be used most effectively in classroom instruction; determining how federal programs in bilingual education can be improved. The twenty-odd projects authorized under this research program involve over nine million dollars of investment of government revenue. Some of the projects are completed. Some are still in the future. The rest are in partial stages of completion. The majority of contracts for these studies have been awarded to contract research firms, while a few have gone to universities.

EVALUATION RESEARCH

Evaluation research is a special field into which some anthropologists have wandered. It is an interdisciplinary activity that has

journals and professional associations, drawing membership from
many occupational categories: economics, statistics, education, sociology, systems analysis, engineering, consulting, government civil
service, and nonprofit agency service, among others. Project evaluators and project managers are increasingly looking for the skills
anthropologists possess for making contributions to the evaluation
research process. In the area of bilingual education, this is especially true. For example, Stephen Arvisu, an anthropologist, is
principal investigator for an in-depth study of Mexican American
bilingual education projects in California. However, until recently,
evaluation research has been largely dominated by analysts who
deal primarily in aggregate data analysis.

CONDITIONS OF FEDERAL CONTRACT RESEARCH

As previously stated, most evaluation research contracted for by
the government, as illustrated by the case of Development Associates' bilingual education evaluation project, is carried out by consulting firms. The design for research is established by the contracting
agency in its Request for Proposals (RFP). The interested firms,
universities, and other parties submit proposals, and the organization whose proposal comes closest to the agency's design and that
appears to have the capacity, experience, and most cost-efficient
price tag will probably win the contract. (Other factors that may be
taken into account are the problem-solving experience of firms and
the believability of the budget. An unbelievably low budget is as
likely to be rejected as an unbelievably high one.) Unlike other
kinds of scientific research, such as those funded by the National
Institute of Health, National Institute of Mental Health, or National
Science Foundation, this research is rarely designed completely by
the project director, although it must be carried out by the director
after winning the competitive process. Then, the research is carefully monitored at all stages of execution by the funding agency,
usually with substantial input as well from the agency being
evaluated.

Therefore, these projects are influenced by policy decisions in
the RFP stage as well as in the execution stage, including changes

in administration, compromises among organizational entities, and the desire to get useful information. Sometimes, an agency designs an evaluation to maximize support for policies, to justify existing programs, or to take into account the constraints of the decision-making environment of government, including lack of time. These conditions may help to explain why government-sponsored research efforts often diverge from what some academicians perceive as desirable or needed.

One thing should be made clear: the reductionist argument that contracted evaluation research is a rubber stamp for ongoing policies is often not true. Furthermore, such activities that evaluation researcher Lewy, citing Stufflebeam, has called "pseudo-evaluation" are dangerous to both the evaluator and the agency (1980:3). Lewy warns that the validity of evaluation results are important not only for ethical reasons but also for maintaining the credibility of the evaluator, and are just as important as serving a paying clientele and meeting their needs in a positive spirit. We strongly advocate the position that valid results are useful and, in the long run, politically powerful for the client agency. But it is incumbent upon the evaluator to convince the client decision makers of the utility of the information. Negative findings must always include suggestions for alternatives.

EVALUATION RESEARCH IN BILINGUAL EDUCATION

In the specific area of evaluation research on bilingual education, there has been a recent trend, especially in research funded by the National Institute of Education (NIE), toward less quantitative and more qualitative evaluation research. What we mean by qualitative evaluation research is that which utilizes in-depth case histories, participant observation, videotaping, mapping, or other methods that are frequently, but not exclusively, associated with the approach anthropologists take toward understanding cultural processes.

We believe that the shift from so-called empirical and/or quantitative research methods toward naturalistic, ethnographic techniques has been required by the fact that the quantitative data and analysis so far generated have not been able to meet the needs of Congress and the bureaucracy for information about the value of bilingual education programs and projects. In other words, by counting types of programs and numbers of beneficiaries, analysts still do not measure what useful learning is taking place in bilingual settings that is not taking place in nonbilingual settings. Understanding and measuring useful learning are difficult to do well but are essential for really useful quantitative data to be generated. Learning, after all, is a holistic process involving a body of information, skills or knowledge, an interaction of teachers with their training, the innate potential of the children, the constraints of the community and home environments, and the attitudes of teachers, children, and parents toward the value of the whole process.

Assuming that quantitative data were correctly generated, it needs to be put into context, because the social value of bilingual education may not be measurable in gross, aggregate statistics on improvement in nationally administered tests. Indeed, the value of bilingual programs seems to lie in the nuances of alterations of identity, self-esteem, and satisfaction that can enhance a positive learning experience.

Quantitative studies, on a grand scale, can often take too long for data accumulation, processing, and analysis to provide necessary information for policy makers. Therefore, changes may not be forthcoming from studies that take too long to fit into the decision-making framework. This critique can be applied equally to qualitative analyses. Ethnographers also frequently conduct time-consuming in-depth studies. Both types of methods need to be modified to meet the time constraints of government decision making. A case in point is the Development Associates' study discussed below, which incorporates both approaches.

Another major constraint in the conduct of evaluation research is that researchers in such evaluation projects have little control over why the research is done. Second, methods, data collection, and analysis techniques are often arrived at by a process of negotiation and consensus rather than by the expert decision of the principal investigator. Finally, the future awarding of contracts is often based on whether the research product met the political and survival needs of the agency and its personnel. Agencies need recommendations for concise, clear-cut decisions, rather than more abstract, noncommittal, and perhaps detailed interpretations of complex situations, which lack the direction needed for implementing concrete changes.

FEDERAL BILINGUAL EVALUATION RESEARCH: CURRENT PROJECTS

The federal government is currently funding a wide variety of research activities on bilingual education programs and their evaluation. The Appendix, below, entitled "Summary of Types of Research in Bilingual Education Funded by Federal Agencies," lists projects identified in two documents dated 1979 concerning proposed levels of funding for projects. This list is provided to give the reader a sense of the types of projects and the 1979 funding proposals for their support. It should be emphasized that these amounts are totals for the life of the project and not for one year alone.

A brief look at the characteristics of the methods used or proposed for these twenty-six projects shows that nine of them incorporate techniques typically used by anthropologists: sociolinguistics, ethnography, in-depth case studies, site visits, and interviewing. These nine projects include the three largest funding amounts totaling 8.7 million dollars. The other seventeen projects can be divided into six low-budget planning studies and eleven studies in which survey research, quantitative analysis, and demographic techniques predominate. A number of those might profit from the incorporation of anthropological methods, at least in part.

The main purpose of presenting this information in this paper is to acquaint the anthropological public with the diversity of types of research efforts and the techniques now being considered as ways of getting at the useful information.

THE DEVELOPMENT ASSOCIATES PROJECT

Cárdenas is the principal investigator of the project appearing in the Appendix under Type III, number 1: Evaluation of the Classroom Instruction Component of the ESEA Title VII Bilingual Education Program. This project was contracted by the Office of Education to evaluate the Basic Projects in bilingual education that are administered by the Office of Bilingual Education and Minority Language Affairs (OBEMLA). These basic projects are distinct from support service projects, training projects, materials development projects, and fellowship programs, all of which may be evaluated separately. Basic projects are awarded to local educational agencies (known as LEAs), institutions of higher education applying jointly with one or more LEAs, or schools operated by the Bureau of Indian Affairs (BIA). This study is limited to projects serving children in kindergarten to grade six. The study, which will cost over 1.5 million dollars, will run until September 1982.

This study is divided into several approaches. In order to determine the characteristics of the extremely varied bilingual education programs now existing in the United States, including almost one hundred languages and many classroom and grade configurations, it is necessary to triangulate various methods. Therefore, the first phase of this study is a survey of some project personnel from all grant recipients. Two questionnaires have been mailed to two different individuals among the project personnel at each of the more than four hundred 1980–81 grant recipients of the Title VII basic projects program. The results from the questionnaires are expected to provide a backdrop or canvas against which subsequent analysis can be arrayed. Also, such a census approach will better depict the broad outlines of the total 1980–81 program. A second phase of data collection will take place this spring when fieldworkers will conduct in-depth interviews in a sample of sixty sites. The interviewers (all trained, permanent staff of Development Associates and Abt Associates, its subcontractor) will carry out structured interviews with school district personnel, school administrators, teaching personnel, and representative parents. All of these data will be synthesized to provide an in-depth look at local program operations. The mail survey and the in-depth interviews will provide data that can be analyzed to describe the implementation of projects, to define major characteristics of projects, and to determine local project objectives.

However, bilingual education does not translate itself easily into tables of numbers or graphs of comparable elements. For example, the sudden influx of large numbers of non-English-speaking students into an area may call for a reorientation of objectives in an already funded project. The changing participation (or lack of it) of parents in a project may seriously modify the nature of classroom instruction during the course of a year. The amount or kind of support from other teachers not directly connected with the project can have serious implications for the design of instruction. These and many other factors can be important for the purpose of defining a project and for understanding the process of implementation. Therefore, many types of data are needed to properly describe and evaluate basic projects. Fieldworkers will conduct on-site observations of classrooms. They will also ask project personnel for access to documents that provide information on the nature of the curriculum, personnel preparation and training, and school policies affecting bilingual education, including materials that guide parent/teacher meetings. From all these sources, case histories of individual projects will be drawn up to illustrate the sixty projects.

But even these efforts may prove to be insufficient for detailing the cultural aspects of the bilingual education process in a school. Some questions that may remain unanswered are the following: (1) What are the various relationships that impede or enhance progress in a project? (2) What are the school values that seem to define the direction of a bilingual education project? (3) What is the significance of the community and its target groups to the bilingual project? (4) Who are the major actors/agencies that have contributed to the project?

In order to provide an accurate response to these and similar questions, the study will conduct individual ethnographies of ten projects selected from among the sixty. Obviously, within the time constraints and the resources available, the study cannot afford to spend unlimited time gathering information on-site for case studies. But the case-study writers will have at their disposal all of the site-specific material from the mailed survey, the results of the on-site interviews, and the various site reports and documents submitted by other fieldworkers. Through these methods, a synthesis will be obtained that is expected to provide both program-wide information and generalizations as well as in-depth analysis of several illustrative projects.

OTHER RESEARCH WITH ETHNOGRAPHIC CONTENT

Other evaluation research projects are now being carried out. Under the aegis of NIE, ethnographic studies are being undertaken to determine the way bilingualism is supported and maintained by parents. The role of communities in the maintenance of bilingualism, and how this impacts or influences local bilingual education projects, is also the objective of other ethnographic studies being implemented in Navajo, Chinese, and Mexican American communities. Another more massive attempt is also being sponsored by NIE, and will require a long-term treatment of on-site observation of classroom behavior. For this study, eight schools with bilingual projects will be selected, and the significant features of instruction will be first identified and then analyzed. The study is referred to below as the Significant Features Study.

FEDERAL POLICY DIRECTIONS

Of course, anthropological approaches have been funded previously, and it is hoped that they will continue to be supported. Nevertheless, researchers should take into account the following trends that indicate directions for the near future.

1. Budget constraints will require a growth in collaborative research efforts among agency researchers, applied practitioners, and basic researchers to maximize the impact of research funds.
2. Federal guidelines will continue to present difficulties to local projects in operational compliance owing to inherent policy contradictions and short-term changes.
3. Basic research that does not look to the practical contexts of bilingual education projects will continue to be irrelevant to teachers struggling with diverse language-related problems.
4. NIE's Significant Features Study will probably generate interest

in the practical classroom techniques to be identified; these may be replicated.

5. The program evaluation aspects of the federal research efforts may be reoriented to include more practical recommendations in three areas: implementation of projects, appraisal of outcome, and assessment of alternatives.

6. The current emphasis on short-term, policy-relevant studies will continue. This may decrease the latitude and flexibility that ethnographic researchers desire. Researchers will need to justify methods on a cost-benefit basis.

7. Studies that justify and/or explain ongoing programs will continue to be needed.

8. Studies aimed at advancing knowledge per se will need to have strong, practical justifications of their utility.

9. The debate over transitional bilingual education versus bilingual education aimed at maintenance has not been resolved. The decision may continue to be left to local educators and the courts.

10. The priorities of educators may continue to be given lower priority than the studies of program operational characteristics by federal efforts.

ADVICE FOR RESEARCHERS
INTERESTED IN FEDERAL AGENCIES

The following recommendations would be well taken by any researcher contemplating seeking federal funding for evaluation research efforts.

1. *Study the client agency.* Approach the federal agency as a complex social system. When dealing with it, learn about its administrative patterns, its relationship to other offices, and especially learn its funding language.

2. *Advocate for beneficiaries and their culture.* Be a clear and honest interpreter of the project beneficiaries' attitudes and perceptions. Translate these into creative and practical suggestions for improvements in program effectiveness and costs savings.

3. *Write clear research designs.* Learn how to describe methods in a task-oriented way. Anthropologists are often too mystical about exactly what they do and how long it takes to do it. Define specific activities in terms of days (or hours) of work. Define specific intermediate and final products that will be of utility to the agency contracting the research as well as to the agency being evaluated. Examples,

such as lists, schedules, protocols, interim reports, maps, diagrams, charts, tables, and final report, can be helpful.

4. *Express opinions.* Concentrate on developing reasonable, informed opinions based on data. Often, academics are afraid to voice opinions on paper when they are not 100-percent certain. The caveats, lacunae, and data-gathering problems tend to dominate their reports and to undermine their credibility. Government officials need to make decisions whether or not the latest fact is inscribed in the field notebook. Research must be done promptly and written up on time and in simple language.

5. *Write executive summaries of your reports.* In these times of personnel cutbacks, agency employees simply do not have the time to read every word of everything that crosses their desks. The executive summary is the key to the impact of any report submitted to the government.

6. *Collaborate on teams.* The verbal exchanges and interactions a researcher has with bureaucrats and local communities should convey understanding and respect for all parties. Researchers are cultural brokers, and need to be very flexible in the multiple contexts in which they work. Researchers also need to learn the vocabulary and analytical terminology of other experts who are part of such projects. In bilingual education projects, these other experts often include economists, planners, educators, administrators, and sociologists.

We hope that these recommendations will help researchers to be more effective in dealing with federal agencies. In that way, anthropologists will have greater likelihood of success in pursuing evaluation research funding for bilingual education.

Summary of Types of Research in Bilingual Education Funded by Federal Agencies

Type I. Assessing the National Need for Bilingual Education

Projects	Implementation Status	Funding	Agencies	Methods	Contractor (if known)
1. Counts of Children	*FY 81	$ 214,000	NCES & NIE	Quantitative (census, survey, and school data)	Bureau of the Census
2. Alternative Methods to Obtain Counts	FY 80	$ 75,000	NCES, OBE, & ASE	Planning projections on methods of counting	
3. Projections of LEP Persons	FY 79	$ 154,283	NCES	Population projection using existing data	InterAmerican Research Associates
4. Adaption of Earlier Measure of English Proficiency	FY 82	$ 25,000	NCES	Developing an analytical procedure for census data	
5. Development of Cost Model for Delivery of Bilingual Services	FY 80	$ 50,000	NCES & NIE	Development of cost model	The Rand Corporation
6. Update of Current National Data on Teacher Language Skills	FY 81	$ 587,962	NCES	Teacher responses to national questionnaire—sample	InterAmerican Research Associates
7. Need for Bilingual Education Training in Puerto Rico	Contract Phase I only	$ 59,263	ASE, NCES, NIE, & OBE	Planning study with analysis of existing data (homeroom census, surveys of immigrants, student records, and test results)	Lourdes Miranda & Associates

*FY = Fiscal Year when funding is completed.

Summary of Types of Research in Bilingual Education Funded by Federal Agencies (cont.)

Projects	Implementation Status	Funding	Agencies	Methods	Contractor (if known)
Type II. Improvement in the Effectiveness of Services for Students					
1. Planning Study of Significant Instructional Features in Bilingual Education Programs	FY 79	$ 198,121	NIE, OBE, & NCES	Case studies, ethnography descriptive studies of classrooms	Abt Associates Inc.
2. Title VII In-Service Training Needs Assessments, Processes, and Activities	FY 80	$ 50,000	OBE	Sample study of proposals from school districts for Title VII funds	
3. Parental Involvement in Bilingual Education Programs	FY 79	$ 310,300	OED & OBE	Descriptive field studies of roles played by parents, perceptions, school records. Generate hypotheses to proceed with in-depth case studies	Systems Development Corporation
4. Development and Dissemination of Instructional Models	FY 79	$ 25,000	ASE, OBE, & NIE	Secondary analysis of existing data	Chess and Associates, Inc.
5. Development and Dissemination of Evaluational Data-Gathering Models	FY 81	$ 410,000	ASE, OBE, & ASPE	Analysis of interviews with program managers and policy makers. Using program documents and operational data	InterAmerican Research Associates

6. Development of Evaluation Models for ESEA Title VII Bilingual Education Projects	FY 80	$ 203,708	OED	Interviews collected from local education agency staff and the results of evaluability assessments	Southwest Regional Laboratory
7. Support of Field-Initiated Proposals for Research on Bilingual Education	Three awards made as of 1979	$ 200,000	NIE	Funding for modest proposals from the field (school districts)	Huron Institute; and others

Type III. Improvement in Title VII Program Management and Operations

1. Evaluation of the Classroom Instruction Component of the ESEA Title VII Bilingual Education Program	Contract awarded	$1,566,984	OED	Survey research coupled with on-site visits and case studies of projects (100 languages)	Development Associates Inc.
2. Development and Installation of a Title VII Program Data System	FY 80	$ 22,000	OBE, ASPE, OED, NIE	Development of data system using program and operation data and survey data	Pinkerton Computer Consultants
3. Feasibility Study of Conversion of Title VII to a Formula-Based Program	FY 81	$ 75,000	NCES & ASE	Planning study using existing data (census etc.)	Applied Urbanetics Inc.
4. Quick-Response Management Studies	FY 81	$ 730,000	ASE & OBE	Planning studies with survey of the literature, interviews of field personnel, and preparation of scopes of work for future research	Various

Summary of Types of Research in Bilingual Education Funded by Federal Agencies (cont.)

Projects	Implementation Status	Funding	Agencies	Methods	Contractor (if known)
5. Impact of Title VII-Funded Training Programs Operated by Institutions of Higher Education	FY 80	$ 511,715	OED, OBE, & NCES	Survey via questionnaire, structured interviewing, analysis of secondary data	RMC Research Corporation
6. Study of the Impact of Title VII Capacity-Building Thrust	FY 80	$ 80,000	OBE & OED	Unknown	

Type IV. Miscellaneous Projects

Projects	Implementation Status	Funding	Agencies	Methods	Contractor (if known)
1. Hispanic Supplement to National Longitudinal Study "High School and Beyond"	FY 82	$ 360,000	NCES Office of Civil Rights	Survey research	National Opinion Research Center
2. Center for Bilingual Research	Awarded	$4,000,000	NIE	Establish and fund a research center	Southwest Regional Laboratory
3. Community and School Interactions (Asian, Native American, and Mexican American Populations)	FY 78	$ 700,000	NIE	Ethnography and sociolinguistic methods	Various

4. Assessing the Language Proficiencies of Bilingual Persons	FY 81	$ 32,966	NIE	Study of proficiency in both first and second language
5. In-Service Teacher Training for Bilingual Education	FY 81	$ 84,904	OED	To determine research and training methods in the form of grants to LEAs (local educational agencies)

Sources: Proposed Research Plan for Bilingual Education, Department of Health, Education and Welfare, July 1979.
Proposed Research Plan for Bilingual Education 1979–1983: Part C Research Agenda Status Report, October 1979 NCBE FORUM, December 1979.

Note. Funding amounts come from proposed levels in July 1979, not actual levels contracted.

References

Academy for Educational Development, 1977. *Paraguay Education Sector Assessment, 1977* (Washington, D.C.: Academy for Educational Development).

ACLO, 1972. *Estudio Socio-económico de las Provincia Belisario Boeto, Chuquisaca* (Sucre: ACLO y Comité de Desarrollo y Obras Públicas de Chuquisaca). [Cited in Albó, Javier, *Lengua y Sociedad en Bolivia 1976* (La Paz: Instituto Nacional de Estadística, 1980).]

Acosta, Robert, and George Blanco, 1978. *Competencies for University Programs in Bilingual Education* (Washington, D.C.: Department of Health, Education, and Welfare, U.S. Government Printing Office).

Albó, Javier, 1980. *Lengua y Sociedad en Bolivia 1976* (La Paz: Instituto Nacional de Estadística).

American Institutes for Research, 1977. *Evaluation of the Impact of ESEA Title VII Spanish/English Education Program, Volume I: Study Design and Interim Findings*, ERIC ED 138 090, Palo Alto, Ca.

Angulo Gallinate, Héctor, Julio Cesar Crespo Rodríguez, Horacio Ulibarrí Montaño, José Rojas Trujillo, Oswaldo Trujillo Ferrufino, Gualberto Tapia Tapia, Máximo Sanabria Ortuño, 1980. *Informe Complementario de Evaluación Institucional del P.E.R.–I* (Cochabamba: Ministerio de Educación y Cultura/Proyecto de Desarrollo Educativo Rural–I).

Asuncion-Landé, Nobleza, 1971. Multilingualism, Politics, and "Filipinism." *Asian Survey* 11(7):677–92.

Aukerman, Robert C., 1971. *Approaches to Beginning Reading* (New York: John Wiley and Sons).

Bailey, Beryl, 1966. *Jamaican Creole Syntax* (Cambridge: Cambridge University Press).

Barry, Jack, 1958. The Making of Alphabets. In *Proceedings of the VIII International Congress of Linguistics*, Eva Siversten, ed. (Oslo: University Press), pp. 752–64.

Bissell, Joan S., 1979. *Program Evaluation as a Title VII Management Tool* (Los Alamitos, Ca.: SWRL Education Research and Development).

Blount, Ben G., 1981. Elicitation Strategies in Parental Speech Acts. In *Child Language: An International Perspective*, P. Dale and D. Ingram, eds. (Baltimore: University Park Press), pp. 241–56.

Blount, Ben G., and W. Kempton, 1976. Child Language Socialization: Parental Speech and Interaction Strategies. *Sign Language Studies* 12:251–77.

Blount, Ben G., and E. Padgug, 1977. Prosodic, Paralinguistic, and Interactional Features of Parent-Child Speech. *Journal of Child Language* 4:67–86.

Bolinger, Dwight, 1964. Around the Edge of Language: Intonation. *Harvard Educational Review* 34:282–93.

Borley, Clive, 1978. *Nelson's New West Indian Readers: Infant Book 1* (Hong Kong: Thomas Nelson and Sons).

Bourricaud, François, 1967. *Cambios en Puno* (México, D.F.: Instituto Indigenista Interamericano).

Boynton, Sylvia, 1980. *Análisis Contrastive de la Fonología del Aymara y del Castellano*, transl. by Pedro Plaza Martínez (La Paz: Instituto Nacional de Estudios Lingüísticos).

Briggs, Lucy Therina, 1976. *Dialectal Variation in the Aymara Language of Bolivia and Peru* (Ph.D. diss., University of Florida).

———, 1979. A Critical Survey of the Literature on the Aymara Language. *Latin American Research Review* 14(3):87–105.

———, 1982. Understanding the Role of Language in Bilingual Education. In *Bilingual Education Teacher Handbook: Language Issues in Multicultural Settings*, Martha Montero, ed. (Cambridge, Mass.: Evaluation, Dissemination, and Assessment Center).

Brinkley, Frances Kay, 1978. An Analysis of the 1750 Carriacou Census. *Caribbean Quarterly* 24:44–60.

Brophy, J. E., and T. L. Good, 1974. *Teacher-Student Relationships* (New York: Holt, Rinehart and Winston).

Bruck, Margaret, Jeffrey Shultz, and Flora V. Rodríguez-Brown, 1979. Assessing Language Use in Bilingual Classrooms: An Ethnographic Analysis. In *Evaluating Evaluation, Bilingual Education*, vol. 6, A. D. Cohen, M. Bruck, and F. V. Rodríguez-Brown, eds. (Arlington, Va.: Center for Applied Linguistics), pp. 40–56.

Burgos G., Hugo, 1977. *Relaciones Interétnicas en Riobamba* (México, D.F.: Instituto Indigenista Interamericano).

Burry, James, 1979. Evaluation in Bilingual Education. *Education Comment* 6(1):1–14.

Carpenter, Lawrence K., 1974. *Conception and Implementation of the El Cerado Bilingual Education Project* (M.A. thesis, Radford University).

Carter, William E., 1977. Trial Marriage in the Andes? In *Andean Kinship and Marriage*, Ralph Bolton and Enrique Mayer, eds. (Washington, D.C.: American Anthropological Association), pp. 177–216.

Casagrande, Joseph B., 1977. Looms of Otavalo. *Natural History* 86(8):48–59.

Casambre, Nelia G., 1978. Language Teaching and Language Standardisation. In *Papers from the Conference on the Standardisation of Asian*

Languages, Manila, Philippines, A. Q. Perez, A. O. Santiago, and Nguyen Dang Liem, eds. (Canberra: Pacific Linguistics), pp. 287–96.

Center for Applied Linguistics, 1974. *Guidelines for the Preparation and Certification of Teachers of Bilingual Bicultural Education.* Reprinted in *Bilingual Schooling in the United States*, T. Andersson and M. Boyer, eds. (Austin, Texas: National Educational Laboratory Publishers, rpt. 1978), pp. 295–302.

Chavez, Leo R., II, 1979. Wedding Day Blues: Class Differences and Social Drama in Otavalo. (Paper presented at the 78th annual meeting of the American Anthropological Association, Cincinnati, O.)

Cohen, Andrew D., 1975. *A Sociolinguistic Approach to Bilingual Education* (Rowley, Mass.: Newbury House).

———, 1979. Bilingual Education for a Bilingual Community: Some Insights Gained from Research. In *Bilingual Education and Public Policy in the U.S.*, R. V. Padilla, ed. (Ypsilanti: Eastern Michigan University), pp. 245–59.

———, 1980a. *Describing Bilingual Education Classrooms: The Role of the Teacher in Evaluation* (Rosslyn, Va.: National Clearinghouse for Bilingual Education).

———, 1980b. *Testing Language Ability in the Classroom* (Rowley, Mass.: Newbury House).

———, n.d. Researching the Linguistic Outcomes of Bilingual Programs. In *The Futures of Bilingual Education: Interdisciplinary Perspectives*, H. T. Trueba, ed. (Rowley, Mass.: Newbury House), in press.

Cohen, Andrew D., and Charles L. Roll, 1979. Assessing Bilingual Speaking Skills: In Search of Natural Language. In *Evaluating Evaluation, Bilingual Education*, vol. 6, A. D. Cohen, M. Bruck, and F. V. Rodríguez-Brown, eds. (Arlington, Va.: Center for Applied Linguistics), pp. 6–21.

Collier, John, Jr., and Aníbal Buitrón, 1949. *The Awakening Valley* (Chicago: University of Chicago Press).

Consejo de Racionalización Administrativa (CRA) and Academia para el Desarrollo Educativo (Academy for Educational Development, AED), 1975. Manual de Introducción a la Problemática de la Escuela Boliviana y la Comunidad Rural de Lengua Vernácula. (Manuscript in the files of Lucy T. Briggs.)

Copana, Pedro, 1981. Linguistics and Education in Rural Schools among the Aymara. In *The Aymara Language in Its Social and Cultural Context: A Collection of Essays on Aspects of Aymara Language and Culture*, M. J. Hardman-de-Bautista, ed. (Gainesville: University Presses of Florida), pp. 255–61.

Craig, Dennis, 1974. Education and Creole English in the West Indies. In *Pidginization and Creolization of Languages*, Dell Hymes, ed. (Cambridge: Cambridge University Press), pp. 371–91.

Cruz, Norberto, Jr., 1979. Parent Advisory Councils Serving Spanish-

English Bilingual Projects Funded under ESEA Title VII. In *Working with the Bilingual Community*, (Rosslyn, Va.: InterAmerican Research Associates), pp. 37–44.

Cummins, James, 1978. Educational Implications of Mother Tongue Maintenance in Minority-Language Groups. *Canadian Modern Language Review* 34(3):395–416.

―――, 1979. Linguistic Interdependence and the Educational Development of Bilingual Children. *Review of Educational Research* 49(2):222–51.

―――, 1980. The Construct of Language Proficiency in Bilingual Education. In *Georgetown University Round Table on Languages and Linguistics, 1980*, James Cummins, ed. (Washington, D.C.: Georgetown University Press), pp. 81–103.

DeAvila, Edward A., and Sharon E. Duncan, 1978. *Research on Cognitive Styles with Language Minority Children: Summary of Pilot Study Design and Data Analysis* (Austin, Texas: Southwest Educational Development Laboratory).

―――, 1979. A Few Thoughts about Language Assessment: The Lau Decision Reconsidered. In *Bilingual Multicultural Education and the Professional*, H. T. Trueba and C. Barnett-Mizrahi, eds. (Rowley, Mass.: Newbury House), pp. 441–53.

DeAvila, Edward A., and Barbara E. Havassy, 1974. Testing of Minority Children: A Neo-Piagetian Alternative. *Today's Education* 63:72–75.

Development Associates, Inc., 1979a. *California Study of Services to LES/NES Students: Interim Report IV* (San Francisco Office).

―――, 1979b. *A Final Report. Bilingual Education Grant Project Paper Development AID/SOD/PDC–C–0193, Bolivia* (Arlington, Va.: Development Associates, Inc.).

―――, 1980. *Final Report. Bilingual Education Project Paper Development. AID/SOD/PDC–C–0193 for USAID Bolivia* (Arlington, Va.: Development Associates, Inc.).

Dilworth, Donald W., and Louisa R. Stark, 1975. Bilingual Education in the Highlands of Ecuador. *Linguistic Reporter* 17(2):3, 5.

Dissemination Center for Bilingual Bicultural Education, 1975. *Evaluation Instruments for Bilingual Education: A Review of Tests in Use in Title VII Bilingual Education Projects* (Austin, Texas).

Dunkin, Michael J., and Bruce J. Biddle, 1974. *The Study of Teaching* (New York: Holt, Rinehart and Winston).

Dyen, Isadore, 1965. *A Lexico-statistical Classification of Austronesian Languages*, Indiana University Publications in Anthropology and Linguistics, Memoir 19.

Educational Daily, 1980. August 15, 1980, pp. 5–6.

Enriquez, Virgilio G., 1978. On the Standardisation of Psychological Terms in Pilipino. In *Papers from the Conference on the Standardisation of*

Asian Languages, Manila, Philippines, A. Q. Perez, A. O. Santiago, and Nguyen Dang Liem, eds. (Canberra: Pacific Linguistics), pp. 207–11.

Escobar, Alberto, 1978. *Variaciones Sociolingüísticas de Castellano en el Peru* (Lima: Instituto de Estudios Peruanos).

Farquhar, Bernadette, 1974. *A Grammar of Antiguan Creole* (Ph.D. diss., Cornell University).

Ferguson, Charles A., 1959. Diglossia. *Word* 15:325–40.

———, 1964. Baby Talk in Six Languages. In *The Ethnography of Communication*, J. Gumperz and D. Hymes, eds. Special Issue, *American Anthropologist*, pt. 2, pp. 103–114.

Fishman, Joshua A., 1967. Bilingualism with and without Diglossia; Diglossia with and without Bilingualism. In *Problems of Bilingualism*, J. MacNamara, ed. *Journal of Social Issues* 23(2):29–38.

Flanders, Ned A., 1970. *Analyzing Teacher Behavior* (Reading, Mass.: Addison–Wesley).

Foley, Douglas E., 1976. *Philippine Rural Education: An Anthropological Perspective* (Northern Illinois University: Center for Southeast Asian Studies).

Fox, James J., 1978. Notes on the Southern Voyages and Settlements of the Sama-Bajau. *Bijdragen* 133(4):459–65.

Frake, Charles, 1957. The Subanun of Zamboanga: A Linguistic Survey. *Ninth Pacific Science Association Congress*, Proceedings 3:93.

———, 1971. Lexical Origins and Semantic Structure in Philippine Creole Spanish. In *Pidginization and Creolization of Languages*, D. Hymes, ed. (London: Cambridge University Press), pp. 223–42.

Frei, Ernest J., 1959. *The Historical Development of the Philippine National Language* (Manila: Institute of National Language).

Friedlander, Judith, 1975. *Being Indian in Hueyapan: A Study in Forced Identity in Contemporary Mexico* (New York: St. Martin's Press).

Gaarder, A. Bruce, 1977. *Bilingual Schooling and the Survival of Spanish in the United States* (Rowley, Mass.: Newbury House).

Galdo Pagaza, Raúl, 1962. *El Indígena y el Mestizo de Vilquechico*, Serie Monográfica No. 9 (Lima: Plan Nacional de Integración de la Población Aborigen).

Gallegos, Luis, n.d. Wancho-Lima, Puno, Peru. (Manuscript in the files of Michael Painter.)

Gonzales, Andrew B., 1978. A First Step toward Standardisation. In *Papers from the Conference on the Standardisation of Asian Languages, Manila, Philippines*, A. Q. Perez, A. O. Santiago, and Nguyen Dang Liem, eds. (Canberra: Pacific Linguistics), pp. 131–66.

———, 1979. Evaluating the Progress of Bilingual Education. *Social Science Information (Philippine Social Science Council, Manila)* 6(4):4–6.

Gonzales, Esperanza, 1975. The 1974 Bilingual Education Policy. (Paper presented at the First Joint National Conference Workshop of Language Supervisors of the Philippines, Silay City.)

Goodenough, Ward H., 1965. Rethinking "Status" and "Role": Toward a General Model of the Cultural Organization of Social Relationships. In *The Relevance of Models for Social Anthropology*, Michael Banton, ed. (London: Tavistock), pp. 1–24.

Goodman, Yetta M., and Carolyn L. Burke, 1972. *Reading Miscue Inventory Manual: Procedure for Diagnosis and Evaluation* (New York: Macmillan).

Goody, Jack, 1976. *Production and Reproduction: A Comparative Study of the Domestic Domain*, Cambridge Studies in Social Anthropology, no. 17. (New York: Cambridge University Press).

Gumperz, John, 1977. Sociocultural Knowledge in Conversational Inference. In *Linguistics and Anthropology*, M. Saville-Troike, ed. (Washington, D.C.: Georgetown University Press), pp. 191–211.

———, 1978. The Conversational Analysis of Interethnic Communication. In *Interethnic Communication*, E. L. Ross, ed. Proceedings of the Southern Anthropological Society, no. 12. (Athens: University of Georgia Press), pp. 13–31.

Gumperz, J., and E. Herasimchuk, 1972. The Conversational Analysis of Social Meaning: A Study of Classroom Interaction. In *Sociolinguistics: Current Trends and Prospects*, R. Shuy, ed. (Washington, D.C.: Georgetown University Press), pp. 99–134.

Hancock, Ian, 1977. Repertory of Pidgin and Creole Languages. In *Pidgin and Creole Linguistics*, Albert Valdman, ed. (Bloomington: Indiana University Press), pp. 362–91.

Hardman-de-Bautista, M. J., 1978. Linguistic Postulates and Applied Anthropological Linguistics. In *Papers on Linguistics and Child Language*, V. Honsa and M. J. Hardman-de-Bautista, eds. (The Hague: Mouton), pp. 117–36.

Hardman-de-Bautista, M. J., and Shoko Saito Hamano, 1981. Language Structure Discovery Methods. (Gainesville, Fla.: mimeographed field manual for students in anthropological linguistics.)

Haugen, Einar, 1956. *Bilingualism in the Americas: A Bibliography and Research Guide* (University: University of Alabama Press).

Hazen, Dan Chapin, 1974. *The Awakening of Puno: Government Policy and the Indian Problem in Southern Peru, 1900–1955* (Ph.D. diss., Yale University).

Hill, Donald R., 1977. *The Impact of Migration on the Metropolitan and Folk Society of Carriacou, Grenada*. Anthropological Papers of the American Museum of Natural History, vol. 54, pt. 2 (New York: American Museum of Natural History).

Hosenfeld, Carol, 1979. Cindy: A Learner in Today's Foreign Language Classroom. In *The Foreign Language Learner in Today's Classroom*

Environment, W. C. Born, ed. (Montpelier, Vt.: Capital City Press), pp. 53–75.

Hosokawa, Koomei, 1980. *Diagnóstico Sociolingüístico de la Región Norte de Potosí* (La Paz: Instituto Nacional de Estudios Lingüísticos).

Hymes, Dell, 1972. Models of the Interaction of Language and Social Life. In *Directions in Sociolinguistics: The Ethnography of Communication*, J. Gumperz and D. Hymes, eds. (New York: Holt, Rinehart and Winston), pp. 38–71.

————, 1974. *Foundations in Sociolinguistics: An Ethnographic Approach* (Philadelphia: University of Pennsylvania Press).

International Bank for Reconstruction and Development (IBRD), 1978. *Bolivia Primer Proyecto de Educación y Formación Profesional Documentos de Trabajo. Educación Primaria y Comunitaria.* División de Proyectos de Educación, Oficina Regional de América Latina y el Caribe, Banco Mundial (Washington, D.C.: IBRD).

Isbell, Billie Jean, 1974. Parentesco Andino y Reciprocidad. Kuyaq: Los Que Nos Aman. In *Reciprocidad e Intercambio en los Andes Peruanos*, Giorgio Alberti and Enrique Mayer, eds. (Lima: Instituto de Estudios Peruanos), pp. 110–52.

————, 1978. *To Defend Ourselves: Ecology and Ritual in an Andean Village* (Austin: University of Texas Press).

Jacobson, Rodolfo, 1979. Can Bilingual Teaching Techniques Reflect Bilingual Community Behaviors? A Study in Ethnoculture and Its Relationship to Some Amendments Contained in the New Bilingual Education Act. In *Bilingual Education and Public Policy in the U.S. Ethnoperspectives in Bilingual Education Research*, vol. 1, R.V. Padilla, ed. (Ypsilanti: Eastern Michigan University), pp. 483–87.

Jakobovits, Leon A., 1970. *A Foreign Language Learning* (Rowley, Mass.: Newbury House).

Kephart, Ronald, 1980. *Preliminary Description of Carriacou Creole* (M.A. thesis, University of Florida).

Labov, William, 1966. *The Social Stratification of English in New York City* (Washington, D.C.: Center for Applied Linguistics).

————, 1969. The Logic of Nonstandard English. *Georgetown Monographs on Language and Linguistics* 22:1–39.

Larson, Mildred L., Patricia M. Davis, and Marlene Ballena Dávila, 1979. *Educación Bilingüe: Una Experiencia en la Amazonia Peruana* (Lima: Instituto Lingüístico de Verano).

Layme, Félix, 1980. *Desarollo del Alfabeto Aymara* (La Paz: Instituto de Lengua y Cultura Aymara).

Leach, Edmund, 1951. The Structural Implications of Matrilateral Cross-Cousin Marriage. *Journal of the Royal Anthropological Institute* 81:24–53.

Lévi-Strauss, Claude, 1969. *The Elementary Structures of Kinship* (Boston: Beacon).

Lewy, Arieh, 1980. Professionals and Their Profession. *Phi Delta Kappa CEDR Quarterly* 13(1):3–6.

Lieberman, Philip, 1980. The Innate, Central Aspect of Intonation. In *The Melody of Language: Intonation and Prosody*, L. Waugh and C. van Schooneveld, eds. (Baltimore: University Park Press), pp. 187–99.

Lounsbury, Floyd G., 1964. The Componential Structure of the Iroquois-type Kinship System. In *Proceedings of the Ninth International Congress of Linguistics*, H.G. Hunt, ed. (The Hague: Mouton), pp. 1073–92.

McDermott, Ray P., 1977. The Ethnography of Speaking and Reading. In *Linguistic Theory: What Can It Say about Reading?*, Roger W. Shuy, ed. (Newark, Del.: International Reading Association), pp. 153–85.

Mamani, Andrés, Lucy T. Briggs, Dionicio Siñani, and Max Catari, 1980. *Informe de Evaluación-Educación Bilingüe. OF–PR–INF–75–80* (La Paz: Ministerio de Educación y Cultura Proyecto Educativo Integrado del Altiplano Crédito 1404–80, MEC/BIRF).

Manuel, Juan D., 1978. Keynote Address. (Presented at the Conference to Assess the Implementation of the Bilingual Education Policy Since 1974, Philippine Normal College, Manila [Cited in A. Gonzales (1979)]).

Marcos, Ferdinand E., 1978. National Language and Unity. In *Papers from the Conference on the Standardisation of Asian Languages, Manila, Philippines*, A. Q. Perez, A. O. Santiago, and Nguyen Dang Liem, eds. (Canberra: Pacific Linguistics).

Maring, Esther G., and Joel M. Maring, 1973. *An Historical and Cultural Dictionary of the Philippines* (Metuchen, N.J.: Scarecrow).

Martin-Barber, Laura, 1975. Phonology. In *Aymar ar Yatiqañataki*, vol. 3, 2d ed., M. J. Hardman-de-Bautista, Juana Vásquez, and Juan de Dios Yapita, eds. (Ann Arbor: University Microfilms International Research Abstracts), pp. 44–107.

Mayer, Enrique, 1977. Beyond the Nuclear Family. In *Andean Kinship and Marriage*, Ralph Bolton and Enrique Mayer, eds. (Washington, D.C.: American Anthropological Association), pp. 60–80.

Meillassoux, Claude, 1975. *Femmes, Greniers et Capitaux* (Paris: Librairie François Maspero).

Miracle, Andrew W., Jr., 1976. The Ethnosemantics of Observable Behavior: Notes on Aymara Social Behavior and Certain Emic Domains. *Florida Journal of Anthropology* 1(2):16–25.

Molony, Carol H., 1969. *Multilingualism and Social Behavior in the Southern Philippines* (Ph.D. diss., Stanford University).

Morse, J. Mitchell, 1980. The Shuffling Speech of Slavery: Black English. In *Exploring Language*, Gary Goshgarian, ed. (Boston: Little, Brown), pp. 269–77.

Múgica Urdangarín, Luis Maria, 1976. *Diccionario Euskara* (Bilbao: Diputación Provincial de Vizcaya).

Otanes, F. T., 1978. The Standardisation of Science Terms in Pilipino. In *Papers from the Conference on the Standardisation of Asian Languages, Manila, Philippines*, A. Q. Perez, A. O. Santiago, and Nguyen Dang Liem, eds. (Canberra: Pacific Linguistics), pp. 179–91.

Pallesen, Kemp, 1978. *Cultural Contact and Language Convergence* (Ph.D. diss., University of California, Berkeley).

Perez, A. Q., A. O. Santiago, and Nguyen Dang Liem, eds., 1978. *Papers from the Conference on the Standardisation of Asian Languages, Manila, Philippines* (Canberra: Pacific Linguistics).

Pineda, Ponciano B. P., 1978. A Dictionary in the Making: Standardisation of Pilipino/Filipino and the Law. In *Papers from the Conference on the Standardisation of Asian Languages, Manila, Philippines*, A. Q. Perez, A. O. Santiago, and Nguyen Dang Liem, eds. (Canberra: Pacific Linguistics), pp. 11–18.

Pletcher, Barbara P., N. A. Locks, D. F. Reynolds, and B. G. Sisson, 1978. *A Guide to Assessment Instruments for Limited English Speaking Students* (New York: Santillana).

Ponce de Léon, Sancho Paz, 1964. *Relación y Descripcíon de los Pueblos del Partido de Otavalo* (Otavalo: Instituto del Indio Americano).

Primer Seminario Nacional de Educación Bilingüe del Ecuador/Shucniqui Tandanacuy Ishcay Shimipi Yachachingapac, 1975. *Documento Final* (Quito: Ministerio de Educación Pública).

Pyle, Ransford C., 1981. Bolivian Bilingual Spanish Phonòlogy. In *The Aymara Language in Its Social and Cultural Context*, M. J. Hardman-de-Bautista, ed. University of Florida Social Sciences Monograph no. 67. (Gainesville: University Presses of Florida), pp. 187–198.

Republic of the Philippines Department of Education and Culture, 1974. *Implementing Guidelines for the Policy on Bilingual Education* (Manila: Office of the Secretary, no. 25, s. 1974).

Republic of Trinidad and Tobago, 1978. *Annual Statistical Digest*, no. 25 (Trinidad and Tobago: Central Statistical Office).

República de Bolivia, 1980. *Código de la Educación Boliviana. Decreto-Ley No. 03937 de 20 de Enero de 1950* (Cochabamba: Editorial Serrano Ltda).

Rivera, Jorge, Alberto Rivera, Juan de Dios Yapita, Gonzalo Flores, Javier Albó, Jorge Dandler, Julio Zúñiga, and Leonardo Yana, 1980. *Social Soundness Analysis Informe Final Proyecto de Educación Bilingüe USAID–Bolivia* (La Paz: Estudio Rivera Ltda).

Rodríguez, Rodolfo, 1979. Community Client Participation in ESEA Title VII Programs: An Inquiry into the Impact of a Federal Mandate. In *Bilingual Education and Public Policy in the U.S. Ethnoperspectives in Bilingual Education Research*, vol. 1, R. V. Padilla, ed. (Ypsilanti: Eastern Michigan University), pp. 260–80.

Rubin, Joan, 1968. *National Bilingualism in Paraguay* (The Hague: Mouton).

————, 1977. Bilingual Education and Language Planning. In *Frontiers of Bilingual Education*, Bernard Spolsky and Robert Cooper, eds. (Rowley, Mass.: Newbury House), pp. 282–94, 326.

Salomon, Frank, 1973. Weavers of Otavalo. In *People and Cultures of Native South America*, Daniel R. Gross, ed. (Garden City, N.Y.: Doubleday/Natural History Press), pp. 463–92.

Sánchez Garrafa, Rodolfo, and Sibylle Riedmiller, 1980. *Bases y Elementos de Planificación del Proyecto Experimental de Educación Bilingüe Puno (Convenio PERU–R.F.A.)* (Lima: Ministerio de Educación, Instituto Nacional de Investigación y Desarrollo de la Educación).

Sapir, Edward, 1921. *Language* (New York: Harcourt, Brace).

Saville-Troike, Muriel, 1978. *A Guide to Culture in the Classroom* (Rosslyn, Va.: National Clearinghouse for Bilingual Education).

Schuchard, Barbara, 1979. *Ñandé Në - Gramática Guaraní para Castellano Hablantes*. Introduction by B. Riester, J. Riester, B. Schuchard, and B. Simon (Lima: Centro de Proyección Cristiana).

Secretaría General de la Organización de los Estados Americanos, 1973. *América en Cifras, 1972: Situación Social* (Washington, D.C.: Organization of American States).

Sibayan, Bonifacio P., 1975. Survey of Language Use and Attitudes in the Philippines. In *Language Surveys in Developing Nations*, Sirarpi Ohannessian, Charles A. Ferguson, and Edgar C. Polomé, eds. (Arlington, Va.: Center for Applied Linguistics), pp. 115–35.

Silliman, Rachel G., 1976. *The Visayans and Pilipino: A Study of Regional Elite Attitudes, Nationalism, and Language Planning in the Philippines* (Ph.D. diss., Claremont Graduate School, Claremont, Calif.).

Silverman, R. J., J. K. Noa, and R. H. Russell, 1976. *Oral Language Tests for Bilingual Students: An Evaluation of Language Dominance and Proficiency Instruments* (Portland, Oreg.: Northwest Regional Educational Laboratory).

Skutnabb-Kangas, Tove, 1979. *Language in the Process of Cultural Assimilation and Structural Incorporation of Linguistic Minorities* (Rosslyn, Va.: National Clearinghouse for Bilingual Education).

Solá, Donald F., and Rose-Marie Weber, 1978. *La Planificación Educativa en Países Multilingües: Un Informe Sobre una Reunión de Trabajo*, Report No. 2 (Ithaca, N.Y.: Cornell University Language Policy Research Program).

Starbird, Ethel, 1979. Taking It as It Comes. *National Geographic* 156(3):399–425.

Stark, Louisa R., 1977a. Proyecto Bilingüe: Castellano-Guaraní, Análisis de Alfabetos (Codificación de Equivocaciones). (Manuscript in the files of the author.)

————, 1977b. *Report: AID Contract 526–416, June 6–July 8, 1977* (Asunción: Agency for International Development).

————, n.d. The History and Current Status of Ecuadorian Highland Quichua. (Manuscript in the files of Lawrence K. Carpenter.)

Stark, Louisa R., and Lawrence K. Carpenter, 1974. *El Quichua de Imbabura: Una Gramática Pedagógica* (Quito: Imprenta y Ediciones Lexigrama).

Stocks, Anthony, 1978. *The Invisible Indians: A History and Analysis of the Relations of the Cocamilla Indians of Loreto, Peru, to the State* (Ph.D. diss., University of Florida).

Troike, Rudolph C., and Nancy Modiano, eds., 1975. *Proceedings of the First Inter-American Conference on Bilingual Education* (Arlington, Va.: Center for Applied Linguistics).

Trueba, Henry T., 1979. Bilingual-Education Models: Types and Designs. In *Bilingual Multicultural Education and the Professional*, H. T. Trueba and C. Barnett-Mizrahi, eds. (Rowley, Mass.: Newbury House), pp. 54–73.

Tucker, G. Richard, and Gary A. Cziko, 1978. The Role of Evaluation in Bilingual Education. In *Georgetown University Round Table on Languages and Linguistics 1978*, J. E. Alatis, ed. (Washington, D.C.: Georgetown University Press), pp. 423–46.

U.S. Department of Health, Education, and Welfare, 1979. *Proposed Research Plan for Bilingual Education* (Washington, D.C.: Office of Assistant Secretary for Education, Education Division, U.S. Printing Office).

Venezky, Richard L., 1970. Principles for the Design of Practical Writing Systems. *Anthropological Linguistics* 12(7):256–70.

Villavicencio, Gladys, 1973. *Relaciones Interétnicas en Otavalo-Ecuador* (México, D.F.: Instituto Indigenista Interamericano).

Walters, Joel, 1980. Language Variation as a Tool in the Assessment of Communicative Competence. In *Proceedings of the Third Annual Conference on Frontiers in Language Proficiency and Dominance Testing*, R. Silverstein, ed. (Carbondale: Southern Illinois University).

Waugh, Linda, and C. H. van Schooneveld, eds., 1980. *The Melody of Language: Intonation and Prosody* (Baltimore: University Park Press).

Weaver, Constance, 1980. *Psycholinguistics and Reading: From Process to Practice* (Cambridge, Mass.: Winthrop).

Webster, Stephen, 1977. Kinship and Affinity in a Native Quechua Community. In *Andean Kinship and Marriage*, Ralph Bolton and Enrique Mayer, eds. (Washington, D.C.: American Anthropological Association), pp. 28–42.

Weil, Thomas E., Jan Knippers Black, Howard I. Blutstein, David S. McMorris, Frederick P. Munson, and Charles Townsend, 1973. *Area Yearbook for Paraguay* (Washington, D.C.: United States Department of State, U.S. Government Printing Office).

Wigginton, Eliot, 1975. *Moments: The Foxfire Experience* (Washington, D.C.: IDEAS).

Willows, Dale M., Diane Borwick, and Maureen Hayvren, 1981. The Content of School Readers. In *Reading Research: Advances in Theory and Practice*, G. E. Mackinnon and T. Gary Waller, eds. (New York: Academic Press), pp. 97–175.

Yapita, Juan de Dios, 1979. *Aymarat Arst'añani. Educación en Lenguas Nativas*, vols. 1 and 2 (La Paz: Instituto de Lengua y Cultura Aymara).

Zuidema, R. T., 1977. The Inca Kinship System: A New Theoretical View. In *Andean Kinship and Marriage*, Ralph Bolton and Enrique Mayer, eds. (Washington, D.C.: American Anthropological Association), pp. 240–81.

The Contributors

BEN G. BLOUNT is professor and chair of the Department of Anthropology at the University of Georgia. His research interests include socialization, communication, language acquisition, and primate social behavior. Areal interests are east and northeast Africa.

LUCY THERINA BRIGGS is visiting assistant professor of Spanish at Dartmouth College. Her research interests include Aymara and Spanish dialectology, the teaching of reading in multicultural settings, and applications of linguistics to language problems and public policy.

RENÉ F. CÁRDENAS is vice-president of Development Associates, Inc., in Arlington, Virginia, as well as project director for two national survey projects—one in bilingual education, and the other on Hispanic health and nutrition. His interests are qualitative aspects of program evaluation, community development, and organizational dynamics.

LAWRENCE K. CARPENTER is a doctoral candidate in anthropological linguistics at the University of Florida. He is currently president and chairman of the board of the Jatari Foundation, involved in Andean education and research. Current research interests include South American indigenous languages, bilingualism, language acquisition of bilinguals, and survival strategies in lowland South America.

ANDREW D. COHEN is associate professor of applied linguistics in the School of Education, Hebrew University of Jerusalem. He is the author of books on bilingual education, bilingual evaluation, and language testing. His current research interest is in making easier second-language learning, and he is using mentalistic measures—for example, introspection—as primary tools in this endeavor.

JANE COLLINS is visiting assistant professor of social sciences at the Georgia Institute of Technology. She recently received her Ph.D. degree in anthropology at the University of Florida after writing her dissertation on kinship and seasonal migration among the Aymara of southern Peru. Her interests are human ecology, kinship, and sociolinguistics.

GABRIEL DeCICCO is associate professor of anthropology at Seton Hall University. Holding a doctorate from the University of Madrid, he has spent most of his career in Spain and Latin America. His interests include both cultural anthropology and linguistics.

NORA C. ENGLAND is associate professor of anthropology and coordinator of the Latin American Studies Program at the University of Iowa. Her major interests are in the description of American languages, literacy, bilingualism, and language policy in Latin America. She has done research on Aymara, Mayan, and Mississippi Choctaw languages, and has taught in a bilingual-teacher-training program for the Mississippi Choctaw. She is currently editor of the *Journal of Mayan Linguistics*.

RONALD KEPHART is a graduate student in anthropology at the University of Florida. He has done linguistic fieldwork in Carriacou, where he previously worked as a Peace Corps volunteer. His primary interests are the structure and sociolinguistics of Caribbean Creole languages.

JOEL M. MARING is associate professor of anthropology at Southern Illinois University in Carbondale. His research interests are in applied linguistics, educational anthropology, and ethnomusicology. With teaching and field research experience in Nigeria, Southeast Asia, New Guinea, and among the Pueblo Indians of the American Southwest, he has published works on the Philippines, Burma, and the Ácoma Keresan Indians.

CHARLOTTE I. MILLER is a social science analyst in the Nutrition Economics Group of the United States Department of Agriculture. Her interests are project design and evaluation, urban anthropology, international development, consumption/nutrition effects of agriculture policies, United States Hispanics, and Brazil and Peru.

ANDREW W. MIRACLE, JR., is associate professor of anthropology at Texas Christian University, where he teaches a course for students in the bilingual education program. His research has focused on various aspects of education, including socialization and schooling among the Aymara.

MICHAEL PAINTER is visiting assistant professor of social sciences at the Georgia Institute of Technology. He received his Ph.D. degree in anthropology from the University of Florida after having conducted doctoral research among the Aymara of southern Peru. His principal areas of interest are economic anthropology and anthropological linguistics.

ROBERT A. RANDALL is assistant professor of anthropology at the University of Houston Central Campus. His primary academic interests include comparative social organization, economic language and cognition, and Southeast Asia. He is the author of *Change and Variation in Samal Fishing: Making Plans to Make a Living in the Southern Philippines*.

LOUISA R. STARK is director of anthropology at the Heard Museum of Anthropology in Phoenix, Arizona. She also holds an appointment as adjunct professor in the Department of Anthropology at Arizona State University. Her major research areas are Latin America and the American Southwest, where she recently has done fieldwork on ethnicity and social stratification.

Index